DEFENSE, SECURITY AND STRATEGY SERIES

OCEAN PIRACY

DEFENSE, SECURITY AND STRATEGY SERIES

Military Satellites: Issues, Goals and Challenges
Abel Chirila (Editor)
2009. ISBN: 978-1-60741-238-0

The Army's Future Combat System Program
Christian N. Feliciano (Editor)
2009. ISBN: 978-1-60741-262-5

Evaluating Military Compensation
Jaime G. Duenas (Editor)
2009. ISBN: 978-1-60741-476-6

Strategizing Resilience and Reducing Vulnerability
Peter R. J. Trim and Jack Caravelli (Editors)
2009. ISBN: 978-1-60741-693-7

Counterinsurgency and the Armed Forces
Laure Paquette
2009. ISBN: 978-1-60741-763-7

National Defense, Security, and Strategy
Norman P. Geise (Editor)
2010. ISBN: 978-1-60692-347-4

Security in Iraq
James L. Jones, Jennifer K. Elsea, and Nina M. Serafino (Editors)
2010. ISBN: 978-1-60692-127-2

U.S. Navy: Operations, Structure and Programs
Colin S. Holmes (Editor)
2010. ISBN: 978-1-60692-124-1

National Security Initiatives
Vivian B. Hickey (Editor)
2010. ISBN: 978-1-60692-354-2

Veterans' Benefits and Care
Mathew H. Bradley (Editor)
2010. ISBN: 978-1-60692-500-3

Misleading Information from the Battlefield
Gene P. Stewart (Editor)
2010. ISBN: 978-1-60741-110-9

U.S. Army on the Mexican Border: A Historical Perspective
Celio Broggini (Editor)
2010. ISBN: 978-1-60876-040-4

Unmanned Aircraft Systems: Strengths and Weaknesses
David G. Casos (Editor)
2010. ISBN: 978-1-60741-114-7

U.S. Military at Sea: Studies on Sea Basing and Navy Crew Rotation
Dominic E. Côté (Editor)
2010. ISBN: 978-1-60741-443-8

U.S. Nuclear Stockpile: Maintenance and Replacement of Warheads
Robin A. Kraemer (Editor)
2010. ISBN: 978-1-60741-483-4

Alternatives for Military Space Radar
Cale M. Gillen (Editor)
2010. ISBN: 978-1-60741-485-8

Recruiting, Retention and Future Levels of Military Personnel
Emmanuel D. Chapman (Editor)
2010. ISBN: 978-1-60741-514-5

War in Afghanistan: Strategy, Military Operations and Congressional Issues
Easton H. Ussery (Editor)
2010. ISBN: 978-1-60741-579-4

Electronic Warfare
Adam T. Elsworth (Editor)
2010. ISBN: 978-1-60741-802-3

Border Security and Who is Responsible for It
Nevio Graziano (Editor)
2010. ISBN: 978-1-60741-804-7

Protest and Issues Around the Air Force Refueling Tanker
Walter P. Zeine (Editor)
2010. ISBN: 978-1-60741-980-8

Transforming the National Guard and Reserves into a 21st Century Operational Force
Jan B. Harkin
2010. ISBN: 978-1-60876-037-4

Special Operations Forces: Background and Issues for the U.S. Military's Elite Units
Adrian Bessette (Editor)
2010. ISBN: 978-1-60741-621-0

Ocean Piracy
Jacob E. Nelson (Editor)
2010. ISBN: 978-1-60741-495-7

National Security: Institutional Approaches, Policy Models and Global Impacts
Nelson J. Patten and Bryce C. Nugent (Editors)
2010. ISBN: 978-1-60876-893-6

Options for Deploying Missile Defenses in Europe
Melissa V. Jordan (Editor)
2010. ISBN: 978-1-60741-889-4

Options for Deploying Missile Defenses in Europe
Melissa V. Jordan (Editor)
2010. ISBN: 978-1-61668-657-4
(Online book)

Biosafety and Biosecurity Issues in High-Containment Laboratories
Damon S. Samuels (Editor)
2010. ISBN: 978-1-61668-706-9

Biosafety and Biosecurity Issues in High-Containment Laboratories
Damon S. Samuels (Editor)
2010. ISBN: 978-1-61668-792-2
(Online book)

Sea-Based Ballistic Missile Defense: Background and Issues
Kevin C. Azure (Editor)
2010. ISBN: 978-1-60741-982-2

Sea-Based Ballistic Missile Defense: Background and Issues
Kevin C. Azure (Editor)
2010. ISBN: 978-1-61668-881-3
(Online book)

DEFENSE, SECURITY AND STRATEGY SERIES

OCEAN PIRACY

JACOB E. NELSON
EDITOR

Nova Science Publishers, Inc.
New York

For permission to use material from this book please contact us:
Telephone 631-231-7269; Fax 631-231-8175
Web Site: http://www.novapublishers.com

LIBRARY OF CONGRESS CATALOGING-IN-PUBLICATION DATA

Ocean piracy / editor, Jacob E. Nelson.
p. cm.
Includes index.
ISBN 978-1-60741-495-7 (hardcover)
1. Maritime terrorism--Prevention. 2. Piracy--Prevention. 3. Hijacking of ships--Prevention. I. Nelson, Jacob E.
HV6431.O28 2009
364.16'4--dc22 2009044335

Published by Nova Science Publishers, Inc. ✣ New York

CONTENTS

PREFACE

This book explores the increase in pirate attacks off the Horn of Africa which is directly linked to continuing insecurity and the absence of the rule of law in war-torn Somalia. The absence of a functioning government in Somalia remains the single greatest challenge to regional security and provides freedom of action for those engaged in piracy along the Somali coast. Some observers also have alleged that the absence of coastal security authorities in Somalia has allowed illegal international fishing and maritime dumping to occur in Somali waters, which in turn has undermined the economic prospects of some Somalis and may be providing economic or political motivation to some groups engaged in piracy. The apparent motive of many active Somali pirate groups is profit, and piracy has proven to be a lucrative activity for many thus far. Beginning in January 2009, the Obama Administration signaled its intention to continue working with U.S. partners in the Contact Group on Somalia and the Contract Group on Piracy off the Coast of Somalia. Enhanced diplomatic engagement with Somali Transitional Federal Governmental officials and leaders from the semi-autonomous region of Puntland also will be launched with the aim of encouraging local Somalis to take steps to secure regions where pirates currently enjoy safe havens. This book consists of public documents which have been located, gathered, combined, reformatted, and enhanced with a subject index, selectively edited and bound to provide easy access.

Chapter 1 - This chapter is edited and excerpted testimony by Michael Coulter before the House Armed Services Committee on March 5, 2009.

Chapter 2 - This chapter is edited and excerpted testimony by William E. Gortney before the House Armed Services Committee on March 5, 2009.

Chapter 3 - This chapter is edited and excerpted testimony by Stephen D. Mull before the House Armed Services Committee on March 5, 2009.

Chapter 4 - This chapter is edited and excerpted testimony by Karl Wycoff before the House Armed Services Committee on March 5, 2009.

Chapter 5 - Many Members of 111th Congress are concerned about the sharp rise in pirate attacks in the strategic waterways in the Gulf of Aden off the East coast of Africa. The hijacking of a Saudi Arabia-owned oil tanker, *Sirius Star*, off the coast of Kenya on November 15, 2008, by pirates, and its release after a $3 million ransom payment on January 8, 2009, was another in a series of seizures and releases that have focused worldwide attention on economic and humanitarian threats posed by pirates to the global seafaring community and the smooth flow of international trade. Given the sharp increase in the number of pirate attacks, the cost of transporting cargo in international waters could rise dramatically because of the sharp increase in ocean marine insurance rates for ships transiting the Gulf of Aden. Commercial insurers, for example, could require a special "war risk" insurance premium costing an additional ten of thousands of dollars a day. These additional costs could adversely impact international trade during the current global economic slowdown.

In addition to proposals for military deterrence and diplomatic engagements, policymakers may elect to consider adjustments to the federal statute (Title XII of the Merchant Marine Act of 1936, as amended) that authorizes the federal government to underwrite marine war risk insurance in circumstances such as piracy. Title XII, administered by the U.S. Department of Transportation's Maritime Administration, authorizes the federal government to act as an insurer or reinsurer of last resort to facilitate waterborne commerce should private ocean marine insurance markets not be able to ensure that financial losses due to war risks (and piracy) will be largely covered.

Policymakers may also elect to maintain the status quo on this statutory authority. The property and casualty insurance industry policyholder surplus is calculated to be approximately $505 billion (as of June 2008). Vessel hull and war risk premiums in the U.S. market paid to insurers totaled approximately $350 million in 2007, and the total value of cargo insurance premiums paid in that year was approximately $833 million, according to industry data. Some may contend, as a result, that the insurance industry appears to be financially capable of handling U.S. exposure to the current piracy threat and that the existing policy "backstop" will be adequate.

Chapter 6 - Pirate attacks in the waters off the Horn of Africa, including those on U.S.-flagged vessels, have brought new U.S. and international attention to the long-standing problem of piracy in the region. The International Maritime Bureau (IMB) recorded 111 attacks in the waters off the Horn of Africa in 2008, almost double the number in 2007. As of September 14, 2009, the U.S. State Department reported 156 attacks had occurred in those waters since January 2009, with 33 successful hijackings. Attacks remain concentrated in the Gulf of Aden between Yemen and the northern coast of Somalia and along Somalia's eastern coastline. However, in July 2009, the United Nations Secretary General warned that "as a result of the military presence in the region, pirates have employed more daring operational tactics, operating further seawards, towards the Seychelles, and using more sophisticated weaponry." Pirate attacks continue to threaten commercial shipping and relief shipments bound for East Africa and the Horn, amid a regional humanitarian crisis that experts are calling the worst since 1984.

The increase in pirate attacks off the Horn of Africa is directly linked to continuing insecurity and the absence of the rule of law in war-torn Somalia. The absence of a functioning government in Somalia remains the single greatest challenge to regional security and provides freedom of action for those engaged in piracy along the Somali coast. Some observers also have alleged that the absence of coastal security authorities in Somalia has allowed illegal international fishing and maritime dumping to occur in Somali waters, which in turn has undermined the economic prospects of some Somalis and may be providing economic or political motivation to some groups engaged in piracy. The apparent motive of many active Somali pirate groups is profit, and piracy has proven to be a lucrative activity for many thus far. Ransoms paid to Somali pirates and their supporters, estimated at over $30 million in 2008, may exacerbate ongoing fighting and further undermine security in the region.

The U.N. Security Council issued four resolutions (1816, 1838, 1846, and 1851) in 2008 to facilitate an international response to piracy off the Horn of Africa. At present, Resolution 1851 has authorized international naval forces to carry out anti-piracy operations in Somali territorial waters and ashore, with the consent of Somalia's Transitional Federal Government (TFG). Resolution 1872, adopted May 26, 2009, authorizes member states to participate in the training and equipping of the TFG security forces in accordance with Resolution 1772 (2007). In January 2009, a multilateral Contact Group on Piracy off the Coast of Somalia (CGPCS) was established to coordinate anti-piracy efforts: U.S., NATO, European Union, regional, and other naval forces are currently patrolling near Somalia in coordination with a U.S.-led Task Force.

Some members of the 111th Congress have expressed concern about the threat posed by piracy, and President Obama has stated that his Administration is resolved to halt the growth of piracy in the Horn of Africa region. The Obama Administration has outlined its policy response to the threat of piracy and pledged to continue working through interagency and multilateral coordination and enforcement mechanisms established during the Bush Administration. Most experts believe that the reestablishment of government authority in Somalia is the only guarantee that piracy will not persist or reemerge as a threat. The 111th Congress has explored a range of options to address both the threat posed by piracy as well as its underlying causes, and has sought to influence U.S. policy through oversight of U.S. military operations and diplomatic efforts and through defense and foreign assistance appropriations and authorizations.

Chapter 7 - This chapter is an edited and excerpted United States Maritime Administration publication on Somali Pirate Tactics.

Chapter 8 - In October 2002, the Inter-Governmental Authority for Development (IGAD) launched a peace process designed to end factional fighting in Somalia, led by the government of Kenya. In September 2003, the parties agreed on a Transitional National Charter (TNC). In August 2004, a 275-member Transitional Parliament was inaugurated in Kenya. In October 2004, parliament elected Abdullahi Yusuf Ahmed as the new president of Somalia. In June 2006, the forces of the Islamic Courts Union (ICU) took control of the capital, Mogadishu. During the six-month rule by the ICU, Mogadishu became relatively peaceful, but efforts to bring peace did not lead to a major breakthrough. On December 28, 2006 Ethiopian troops captured Mogadishu with little resistance from the ICU.

The Ethiopian intervention led to more chaos and instability in Somalia over the past two years. Humanitarian, political, and security conditions continue to deteriorate across south-central Somalia. In the past two years, more than 15,000 civilians have been killed, an estimated 1.1 million people displaced, and 476,000 Somalis have fled to neighboring countries. In 2008, fighting between insurgent groups and Ethiopian-TFG forces intensified, and by late 2008, the TFG had lost control of most of south-central Somalia to insurgent groups. In November 2008, the Ethiopian government announced that its forces would pull out of Somalia by the end of 2008. In January 2009, Ethiopian forces completed their withdrawal from Somalia. In late December 2008, President Yusuf resigned from office and left for Yemen.

In June 2008, the TFG and the Alliance for the Re-Liberation of Somalia (ARS), a group dominated by members of the ICU, signed an agreement in Djibouti mediated by United Nations Special Envoy Ahmedou Ould-Abdullah. The parties agreed to a cease-fire, the withdrawal of Ethiopian forces, and the deployment of a United Nations peacekeeping force. Several towns are now administered by the ARS, including Jowhar and Beledweyne. A number of other towns, including the third largest town, Kismaayo, are now under the control of the Al-Shabaab, a group opposed to the TFG and the ARS-Dj ibouti faction. The next phase of the Somali conflict is likely to occur between the ARS and the Al-

Shabaab. In February 2008, Secretary of State Condoleezza Rice designated Al-Shabaab as a Foreign Terrorist Organization. In January 2009, the Somali Parliament elected the leader of the ARS, Sheikh Sharif Sheikh Ahmad as president. In February 2009, President Ahmad appointed Omar Abdirashid Ali Sharmarke as prime minister.

Meanwhile, Somali pirates have intensified their attacks in the Gulf of Aden, carrying out attacks on over 90 commercial ships, and successfully hijacked over 35 ships in 2008. Currently an estimated 14-18 ships are under the control of the pirates, including a Saudi-owned supertanker, *Sirius Star*, and a Ukrainian-owned ship, *MV Faina*, with 33 T-72 tanks and other weapons. In January-February 2009, Somali pirates released a number of the hijacked ships, including the *MV Faina.* The pirates have earned more than $120 million in ransom payments, and have released a number of the ships and crew members. The United States, Russia, India, and several other countries have deployed warships to tackle piracy in the Horn of Africa region. Some insurgent leaders have warned the pirates to end their illegal activities and to release crew members and ships that they currently control.

In: Ocean Piracy
Editor: Jacob E. Nelson
ISBN: 978-1-60741-495-7

Chapter 1

INTRODUCTORY REMARKS BY PDASD(ISA) COULTER TO THE HASC ON MARCH 5, 2009

Michael Coulter

Good morning Chairman Skelton, Ranking Member McHugh, and members of the House Armed Services Committee. Thank you for the invitation to appear before you today to discuss counterpiracy operations in the Gulf of Aden. My name is Michael Coulter and I am the Principal Deputy Assistant Secretary of Defense for International Security Affairs. My office provides defense policy guidance for Europe, Africa, and the Middle East.

In a moment, I'll introduce Vice Admiral Gortney, the naval commander of our military operations in the Gulf of Aden. He will go into the details of our efforts to combat piracy but before he does, I would like to take a brief minute to outline how we see piracy in the broader policy context.

Throughout our history, we have depended on maritime highways for a global transportation system that delivers goods and materials around the world. The concept of unimpeded sea lanes underpins the very meaning of an effective national security strategy... a strategy primarily based on global engagement and to protect and sustain the global, inter-connected, economic system through which we maintain our way of life. Today, freedom of access means the awareness and control of the entire spectrum of the maritime domain to ensure its access to good actors and deny its access to bad actors. From experience, we have come to learn that no one nation can single-handedly secure every ocean and every waterway around the world. And because the oceans play an indispensable role in the safety, security, and economic stability of the international community, all nations have a vital interest in ensuring that the maritime domain remains secure and open for the free and legitimate use of all.

For these reasons, the recent uptick in piracy in the Gulf of Aden has caused like-minded leaders in industry and government to unite to discuss what can done, collectively, to unhinge and defeat the scourge of piracy. We, along with a number of other countries and international organizations, have now committed additional resources to this task. As you will hear from VADM Gortney, we are partnering together with traditional Allies, and with new partners, to achieve international interests. We will, in our collective effort, use the seas to unite and not divide.

The shaping function of this mission must be interagency as well as international. Only some of the tools required to shape the security environment, and to reach into the ungoverned sea spaces, reside in the U.S. or international navies. The root causes of piracy reside on land. The absence of a strong government in Somalia remains the single greatest challenge to regional security and provides freedom of action for those engaged in piracy along the Somali coast. We are therefore reaching out to interagency participants with their tools and even further into the private sectors. The net beneficiaries of these efforts in the international community must also be proud and robust contributors.

The Defense Department co-chairs with the State Department an interagency Counter Piracy Steering Group that addresses the full spectrum of anti- and counter-piracy efforts, from piracy prevention, to interruption and termination of acts of piracy, to ensuring the accountability of pirates. The Defense Department is also supporting the State Department through the recently-established Contact Group on Counter-Piracy off the Coast of Somalia, an international forum that is encouraging countries with a direct interest in countering piracy (including flag and crew States) to provide counter-piracy forces, track piracy financing, and accept custody of and prosecute suspected pirates when apprehended.

Mr. Chairman and members of the committee, thank you again for this opportunity to appear before you today. Now, let me introduce and turn things over to Vice Admiral Gortney. Following Vice Admiral Gortney's comments, I would be happy to take any questions.

In: Ocean Piracy
Editor: Jacob E. Nelson
ISBN: 978-1-60741-495-7

Chapter 2

COUNTER-PIRACY OPERATIONS IN THE U.S. CENTRAL COMMAND AREA OF OPERATIONS

William E. Gortney

Good morning Chairman Skelton, Ranking Member McHugh and members of the House Armed Services Committee. Thank you for the opportunity to testify before you today on our Coalition counter piracy operations in the Central Command area of operation. I appreciate the opportunity to discuss the accomplishments that have been made over the past several months and to identify some of the challenges that lie ahead.

My name is Vice Admiral Bill Gortney, and I am the Commander of U.S. Naval Forces Central Command headquartered in the Kingdom of Bahrain. I took command of NAVCENT at the beginning of July, but have been operationally deployed to the region throughout my Navy career. As the NAVCENT Commander, I am the Naval Component Commander for General Petraeus at U.S. Central Command.

I also command two additional organizations. I serve as the Commander of the United States Fifth Fleet – the Navy's Numbered Fleet Commander. And most importantly in terms of this hearing, I serve as the Commander of the Combined Maritime Forces (CMF) – an international coalition of more than twenty nations who provide people, ships and aircraft in the region. There are national mandates that limit the participation of some of our coalition partners, but this remains a cooperative, multi-national effort. a coalition of the willing.

As most of you know, acts of piracy spiked in late August – but the recent history of piracy doesn't start there. Several years ago we started to see an increase in piracy off the east coast of Somalia. At that time, it was routine for merchant vessels to transit along the coast. In response to those attacks, the shipping industry moved the transit lane further off the coast. It worked, and the rate of attacks decreased – returning to just a few per year.

That changed in August, when a new clan of Somali pirates begin to attack ships in the Gulf of Aden – to the north of Somalia. The number of ships pirated went from three to twelve in just a few days. Ultimately, the solution to the problem of piracy is ashore — in Somalia. I focused the Coalition maritime efforts on security and stability prevention operations at sea that would give the international community time to address the longterm solution.

In late August, as the commander of the CMF – I directed the establishment of a Maritime Security Patrol Area (MSPA) in the Gulf of Aden. We have had coalition ships and aircraft patrolling the area ever since.

The MSPA was just one part of a Counter-Piracy Campaign Plan developed by my staff. The plan was designed to complement and further the efforts of the Political/Diplomatic and Industrial/Maritime communities. The operational design of the plan was developed with the purpose of outlining our efforts to engage the international community along three primary lanes: Political/Legal, Informational/Industrial, and Military.

We focused our counter-piracy efforts on three main areas:

- International Naval Presence
- Improved Defensive Measures from the Shipping Industry
- International Legal Framework for Resolving Piracy Cases

Since late August there have been significant strides made. To date, we have seen forces from the US, UK, Canada, China, Denmark, France, Germany, Greece, India, Italy, Japan, Malaysia, Netherlands, Russia, Saudi Arabia, Spain, Turkey and Yemen. Some of these forces operate within alliances such as NATO or EU, some as part of the CMF coalition and some independently representing their own nation's interests. Additional forces from Japan, Singapore, Republic of Korea, Sweden, Belgium, and Poland are expected to participate in the coming months.

The shipping industry has also been at the forefront. We have seen countless examples of shipping companies, and individual merchant mariners taking proactive measures to serve as the first line of self defense against pirates – these armed criminals operating at sea.

On the operational side of the plan, I initially gave the mission to the Commodore of one of our existing task forces – Combined Task Force (CTF) - 150. However, I did so knowing that it was an additional mission for an already busy operational commander.

More importantly, I did so very carefully – because I knew that some navies in our coalition did not have the authority to conduct counter-piracy operations. We will never ask a member of the coalition to be involved in operations that they do not have the authority from their national authority to do.

As a result of the complexity of the operations in that portion of our Area of Responsibility (AOR), I determined that it was necessary and prudent to establish a separate task force with a specific mission and mandate to conduct counter-piracy operations. In early January we established CTF 151 based on United Nations Security Council Resolutions 1838, 1846 and 1851. The task force was operational by the middle of the month.

Since that time we have had several nations join the task force, and have had formal indications from others who have stated that they will be sending ships and/or aircraft in the coming months. The efforts of CTF-151 are critical to the tactical coordination and deconfliction efforts with all of the international naval forces operating in the Gulf of Aden. We have incredible examples of international cooperation – ranging from personnel exchanges to operational mission coordination to maximize the efficiency of our efforts.

CTF- 151 and other cooperating naval forces have encountered approximately 250 pirates: 130 were disarmed and released, 110 disarmed and turned over for prosecution, and 7 are pending final disposition.

Pirate capacity has been further impacted by the seizure or destruction of 28 pirate vessels, and the confiscation of the pirates' tools of the trade, including: 133 small arms, 28 Rocket Propelled Grenades (RPGs), 51 RPG projectiles, and 21 ladders/grappling hooks.

Ultimately, piracy is a problem that starts ashore and requires an international solution ashore. We made this clear at the outset of our efforts – we cannot guarantee safety in this vast region. Our role in preventing some of these attacks is only one part of the solution to preventing further attacks. Historical precedent can be found in our nation's encounters with the Barbary pirates.

We have been successful not only in our Coalition efforts, but in communicating and coordinating with other naval forces deployed to the region, as well as working with the merchant shipping industry to share lessons learned and best practices.

Lastly, I would like to take a moment to acknowledge the tremendous efforts of the Sailors, Marines, Coast Guard personnel and civilian Navy mariners under the command of Rear Admiral Terry McKnight – the CTF- 151 commander. They have truly made a difference.

Mr. Chairman and members of the committee, I want to thank you for inviting me to appear here today and I will be happy to answer your questions.

Executive Summary

Piracy is a threat to the security of all nations and ultimately requires an international solution ashore. The U.S. Navy leads a Coalition of nations sending ships and aircraft to deter maritime pirate activity, enabling the shipping industry time to implement self- protection measures and the international community to establish a legal framework to hold pirates accountable for their actions.

Ultimately, the solution is in Somalia — assuring security and stability, enacting the rule of law and eliminating the conditions that breed pirates.

The proactive measures being taken by a considerable number of merchant vessels are exactly what we have been recommending. We have been working closely with the commercial shipping industry and the International Maritime Organization to recommend best practices and leverage lessons learned to employ reasonable self-protection measures. We applaud the efforts that the industry has undertaken.

The following is a comprehensive overview of our Coalition, the problem of piracy, and the measures we have undertaken in the maritime environment to help prevent the problem.

1. Background on the Combined Maritime Forces (CMF)

The Combined Maritime Forces is an international coalition consisting of more than 20 nations. Coalition maritime operations are structured along geographic and operational areas of responsibility.

- **CTF 150** conducts Maritime Security Operations (MSO) southeast of the Strait of Hormuz and in the Gulf of Aden, the Gulf of Oman, the Arabian Sea, the Red Sea to the Suez Canal, and portions of the Indian Ocean.

- **CTF 151** was established to conduct counter-piracy operations throughout the CMF area of responsibility. Currently, these operations are focused in the Gulf of Aden with an aim of creating a lawful maritime order and maintaining security in the maritime environment.

- **CTF 152** conducts MSO in the international waters of the Arabian Gulf, and complements the security activities of Gulf Cooperation Council nations in their own territorial waters.

2. Piracy Backgound

The piracy problem emanating from Somalia has grown from the economic, social and political strife that has gripped that country since the mid-1990s. With a government powerless to stop illegal fishing and dumping in the waters off Somalia, local Somali fisherman began taking it upon themselves to deal with the problem by capturing what they perceived as illegal fisherman. The country has no national level military organization.

During recent years, the Darod and Hawiye clans in Somalia have taken to piracy as a means of conducting this sort of 'vigilante' justice as well as to supplement their livelihood by capturing larger, ocean going boats and ships. With the amount of traffic in the Gulf of Aden (GOA) and the ease with which the pirates were able to seize ships, the Darod clan pirates dramatically increased their efforts to capture larger merchant vessels in order to obtain larger ransoms. These clans operate along more than 1800 miles of Somalia coastline.

This increase in activity sharply spiked in August of 2008, prompting greater international interest. The capture of ships with dangerous military cargo like Motor Vessel FAINA and supertankers like the SIRIUS STAR prompted a greater international naval response.

3. The Statistical Information

Piracy impacts less than 1% of shipping. More than 33,000 vessels transit the Gulf of Aden annually, and in 2008 there were 122 attempted attacks, of which 42 were successful and 80 unsuccessful. While this is statistically small, even one attack is too many, and threatens confidence in the safety and reliability of international sea lanes.

To put the challenge into geographic perspective, the area involved off the coast of Somalia and Kenya as well as the Gulf of Aden covers more than 1.1 million square miles, roughly four times the size of Texas.

Of 15 pirate attacks in the Gulf of Aden in late 2008, at least 10 involved ships operating outside the International Maritime Organization's (IMO) recommended traffic corridor or failing to employ recommended self protection measures, making them more vulnerable to a successful attack.

Thus far in 2009 there have been 26 attacks on merchant vessels, with 4 ships being successfully pirated. We believe that the international naval presence, coupled with the efforts of the merchant mariners and the shipping industry – aided in some cases by the weather – has had an impact on the success rate of these pirate attacks. The following are snapshots of piracy in 2008 and thus far in 2009.

2009 Daily Piracy Events Snapshot as of 04 MAR [NAVCENT AOR]

- 26 piracy events
- 4 successful [15 % of the events]
- 22 unsuccessful [85 % of the events]
- 7 suspected pirates currently held by CTF- 151
  - 0 suspected pirates turned over for legal prosecution
  - 9 released based on lack of evidence, positive identification
- 7 ships currently pirated
- Approximately 123 merchant mariners being held hostage

2008 Piracy Events Summary [NAVCENT AOR]

- Estimated 33,000 ships transit the Gulf of Aden annually
- 122 piracy events [0.37% of overall traffic]
- 42 successful [0.13% overall / 38% of the events]
- 80 unsuccessful [62% of the events]

4. COMBINED MARITIME FORCES EFFORTS TO COUNTER PIRACY

The Maritime Security Patrol Area (MSPA)

Our initial response following the August 2008 spike in successful pirate attacks was to establish a presence in the Gulf of Aden using ships and aircraft already working in the region under the command of Combined Task Force 150. We created a Maritime Security Patrol Area (MSPA) to enable warships to work in concert with each other to protect vital shipping in the GOA.

Merchant mariners are being encouraged to transit through the patrol area via Notices to Mariner messages and broadcasts over VHF radio. The have also been asked to share information with naval forces and with their fellow merchant mariners.

Coalition ships are in the area as part of our continual presence in this region. While they have conducted routine operations in the area in the past, the establishment of the MSPA focused efforts to prevent destabilizing activities in the region, while the IMO works the long-term international efforts.

The MSPA was not designed as a specific geographic area, but rather it was established as a moveable area placed atop the existing internationally recognized transit corridor.

This enabled the limited number of warships to protect a greater number of merchant vessels by concentrating them in numbers and in proximity. The MSPA has since proven to be an effective method of de-conflicting the many international warships that are now patrolling the GOA.

Ultimately, the solution to piracy is ashore, and involves removing the conditions which have enabled the pirates to operate with impunity from safe havens along more than 1800 miles of Somali coastline. The designation of the MSPA was originally intended as a near-term effort to allow the international political community time to establish a proper long-term legal framework for dealing with pirates. We also placed a significant emphasis on working with the merchant community identify and implement effective self-protective measures.

Combined Maritime Forces Counter-Piracy Campaign Plan

In order to assist and further the efforts of the Political/Diplomatic and Industrial/Maritime communities, CMF developed a counter-piracy campaign plan. This plan's operational design was developed with the purpose of outlining our efforts to engage the international community along Political/Legal, Informational/Industrial, and Military lines.

We focused our counter-piracy efforts on three main areas:

- International Naval Presence
- Improved Defensive Measures from the Shipping Industry
- International Legal Framework for Resolving Piracy Cases

Most importantly, we articulated that all of these areas must be addressed – none will be successful by itself.

Lessons Learned and Best Practices

We have worked closely with the merchant shipping industry to share the lessons learned and best practices to help merchant mariners more effectively provide the first layer of defense against pirates who would target their vessels.

Some merchant mariners have clearly listened to our recommendations and lessons and have employed reasonable self-protection measures that discourage pirates from attempting to take their vessels. These measures have ranged from proactive lookouts and evasive maneuvering to using charged fire hoses to fend off attackers.

However, we have also recommended that shipping companies embark professional security teams to protect their ships, cargo, and crews. Security teams, whether they employ non-kinetic or kinetic means of deterring pirates add an important layer of defense measures to the equation. We don't have any indications that the pirates are going after specific targets – they are going after the easy targets.

The Establishment of Combined Task Force 151 (CTF-151)

As noted in the introduction, we established Combined Task Force 151 in early January 2009. CTF 151 has been exclusively focused on conducting counter-piracy operations in the Central Command area of responsibility.

Following a growing international naval response, CMF determined that counter-piracy operations required the establishment of a stand alone task force.

CTF-151 was formally established on 1 January 2009, and an initial core staff began to work with the staff of CTF-150 to develop the framework for the new task force. The task force became fully operational in the middle of January.

Establishing CTF-151 cleared up the lines of command. Not all nations participating in CTF-150 had national authorization to conduct counter-piracy operations. This allows coalition nations who have a national mandate to conduct counter-piracy operations to join CTF-151, and those nations without such authority to operate with CTF-150 or CTF-152 with their pre-established Maritime Security Operation mandates.

U.S. Navy Rear Admiral Terence "Terry" McKnight commands Combined Task Force 151.

Counter-piracy operations exemplify the basic principals of the Navy's Maritime Strategy, including: Forward Presence, Deterrence, Sea Control, Power Projection, and Maritime Security.

Tactical and Operational Coordination and Deconfliction

As other nations and organizations like NATO and EUNAVFOR began to send ships to combat piracy, we quickly identified the need to coordinate and tactically de-conflict the efforts of the various task forces. It was imperative from an operational risk management perspective as well as an efficiency of mission perspective. Our forces took the initiative to share unclassified tactical and operational level information with any and all forces in the region conducting counter-piracy operations. The reality is that the vast majority of the material is unclassified.

Direct tactical and operational coordination with NATO and EU forces has led to successful interdiction and capture of suspect pirates, enabled the safe transit of otherwise vulnerable shipping, including World Food Programme ships, effective monitoring and intelligence gathering, as well as enhanced communication among an diverse international naval presence in the Gulf of Aden. To date, forces from the US, UK, Canada, China, Denmark, France, Germany, Greece, India, Italy, Japan, Malaysia, Netherlands, Russia, Saudi Arabia, Spain, Turkey and Yemen have conducted counter-piracy operations. Some of these forces operate within alliances such as NATO or EU, some as part of the CMF coalition and some independently representing their own nation's interests. Additional forces from Japan, Singapore, Republic of Korea, Sweden, Belgium, and Poland are expected to participate in the coming months.

All are in communication with CMF and with each other at some level, and there have been zero safety incidents resulting in injury or death of friendly forces due to lack of effective communication and coordination.

Since implementation of our campaign plan, a number of remarkable positive steps and effects have been achieved. The deployment of the naval forces from all of the nations identified above is a clear indication of the importance of maintaining security in the sea lines of communication.

Shared Awareness and DE-confliction (SHADE) Working Group

CMF has also established SHADE to ensure the various naval forces are working in concert. This is a staff-level group of officers from the various operational headquarters who meet regularly to ensure the naval forces conducting counter-piracy operations are coordinating effectively. The products from this group include the establishment of the Internationally Recommended Transit Corridor (IRTC), and the incorporation of the Fleet Exercise Web (FEXWEB), which is an unclassified internet-based information sharing forum, similar to a chat room. FEXWEB is hosted by the European Union Naval Forces (EUNAVFOR) headquarters in Northwood, UK.

Our Initial Track Record

CMF and other cooperating naval forces have encountered and disarmed approximately 250 pirates: 130 were released, 110 turned over for prosecution, and 7 are pending final disposition.

Pirate capacity has been further impacted by the seizure or destruction of 28 pirate vessels, 133 small arms, 28 Rocket Propelled Grenades (RPGs), 51 RPG projectiles, 21 ladders/grappling hooks, 12 cell phones, and 4 GPS devices.

Despite these results, pirate capacity and number of attempts per month by the pirates have not been significantly reduced. Until the mid- to long-term goals of removing safe havens ashore are achieved, the military presence will be required to be robust. CMF will continue to pursue all elements of the campaign and will continue to seek cooperation, coordination, and de-confliction from all participants.

5. The Costs of Counter-Piracy Operations

U.S. Navy units operating as a part of Combined Task Force 151 are units already deployed to the NAVCENT/FIFTH Fleet Area of Responsibility. Total costs of the task force's counter-piracy operations from its establishment in January through 19 February 2009 are estimated at $1.5 million. These costs include flight hours, steaming days, and supplies.

6. Additional Aspects of Counter-Piracy Operations

The following sections provide additional information on issues related to piracy and CMF counter-piracy operations.

M/V FAINA – from Attack to Release/Humanitarian Support

The Motor Vessel FAINA was attacked off the coast of Somalia on September 25th. The roll-on/roll-off (Ro-Ro) ship is Belize flagged and operated by "Kaalbye Shipping Ukraine." While the ship initially had a crew of 21, the ship's captain reportedly suffered a fatal heart attack shortly after being taken hostage. The pirates refused all requests to turn over the Captain's remains. The ship's remaining crew included 17 Ukrainian citizens, as well as two Russians and one Latvian.

For the more than four months that the ship was pirated, the U.S. Navy maintained a visual watch over this ship as it was anchored just off the Somali town of Hobyo. Assigned ships included the cruiser USS Vella Gulf (CG 72), the destroyers USS Howard (DDG 83) and USS Mason (DDG 87), and the Military Sealift Command's USNS Catawba. Operational support of FAINA was a U.S. Navy-only (vs. Coalition/CTF 150/151) operation, and there were no Coalition naval vessels taking part in this specific mission. This was due to the fact that U.S. ships were under national tasking.

The Norfolk-based destroyer, USS Mason (DDG 87) provided humanitarian assistance support to the crew of the M/V FAINA following the ship's release by Somali pirates. A medical corpsman from Mason checked on the health of the crew, and found them to be in good health. The remains of the ship's Captain were also repatriated.

The U.S. Navy fleet ocean tug USNS Catawba (T-ATF 168) provided logistics support to M/V FAINA and her crew – including fuel and water. USNS Catawba is one of four 226-foot-long fleet ocean tugs operated by the Navy's Military Sealift Command.

Days later, the Captain of the FAINA sent thank you letters to the Captains and crews of the U.S. Navy vessels that had kept watch over the ship. The letters were signed by members of the FAINA crew. Copies of those letters are included at the end of this document.

The Supertanker SIRIUS STAR

On November 15, 2008 the very large crude tanker Sirius Star was attacked more than 450 nautical miles southeast of Mombasa, Kenya. The ship is flagged in Liberia, owned by the Saudi Arabian-based Saudi Aramco, and operated by Vela International. The crew of 25 includes citizens of Croatia, Great Britain, the Philippines, Poland, and Saudi Arabia.

The attack on the Sirius Star set several precedents:

- The ship was the largest pirated in this region: more than 300,000 metric tons, almost three times the tonnage of a Nimitz class aircraft carrier
- It was attacked more than 450 nautical miles southeast of Mombasa, Kenya
- The ship has a freeboard of approximately 10 meters (33 feet)

This SIRIUS STAR attack occurred amid a decrease in the rate of successful pirate attacks on merchant vessels off the coast of Somalia.

The ship was released early on the morning of January 10th, after payment was made via an air drop.

Memorandum of Understanding with Kenya

The United States is consulting with the Government of Kenya about the transfer of suspected pirates for purposes of prosecution in Kenyan courts. However, we're not yet in a position to say where prosecution might take place. There are many possible venues, including the states associated with the victims of these attacks.

Piracy is a universal crime under international law and many states have implemented domestic legislation criminalizing piracy. Moreover, Kenya and the United States have entered into an MOU under which Kenya would prosecute pirates that had been interdicted by U.S. forces.

We are grateful to Kenya in this regard, and want to stress that regardless of where the prosecution takes place, the United States believes that all the affected states must play a role and share the burden in bringing suspected pirates to justice.

Legal Authorities for Holding Suspected Pirates

The legal authority to hold pirates on board a Navy ship is customary and conventional international law, coupled with the recent United Nations Security Counsel Resolutions on Piracy in Somalia (UNSCR 1816, 1838, 1846, 1851). It is customary international law that every State may seize pirate ships and arrest persons suspected of piracy; they must use "warships, or military aircraft or other ships and aircraft clearly marked and identifiable as being on government service and authorized to that effect" to do so. The persons can be held on board the vessels until appropriate arrangements can be made to move them ashore to an appropriate jurisdiction. There is no standard time period requirement.

The suspected pirates have the right to be treated humanely. The pirates' rights with respect to alleged offenses depend on the country that agrees to take them for prosecution. Since piracy is a universal crime, all countries have the right to prosecute them. Whether a particular country has taken steps to create a domestic legal regime for prosecution of piracy and what limitations that regime may have is a separate issue.

We have a number of Somali translators aboard our vessels. We also have basic communication cards with pictures that aid in the communication process.

The task force commander's staff assembles evidence and forwards the material to the legal staff of the Combined Maritime Forces / NAVCENT. The materials will be reviewed, and a recommendation will be made to the Commander, who will determine whether to pursue prosecution or release the individuals. We have embarked security personnel - to include the Naval Criminal Investigative Service - who are experienced in evidence collection and processing.

Each situation is likely to be different. If the vessel they were operating was determined to be sea worthy, suspected pirates may be returned to their vessel -- without their weapons. If their vessel is not sea worthy, we will make arrangements to ensure they are safely repatriated.

Safe and Humane Treatment for Suspected Pirates

Currently suspected pirates are housed onboard USNS Lewis and Clark in two separate converted storage facilities. Each Suspect Pirate is given a foam mat and blanket, as well as coveralls and shoes. They are provided three meals per day, allowed to shower, and issued fresh clothing every other day. Navy medical personnel evaluate their health daily. They are handled with the utmost of care and monitored by United States Marine Corps security personnel who are trained in handling these situations. Our trained Somali translators have been invaluable to facilitate communication

The Presence of International Navies and Their Missions

EU – Operation A TALANTA

As noted previously, our coalition forces work closely with a number of international naval forces deployed to the region to conduct counter-piracy operations. In accordance with Resolutions 1814 (2008), 1816 (2008) and 1838 (2008) of the United Nations Security Council (UNSC), the EU decided to conduct a maritime military operation to contribute to the deterrence, prevention and repression of acts of piracy and armed robbery off the Somali coast and in the broader area.

UNSC Resolution 1838 (2008) of 7 October 2008 commends the ongoing planning process towards a possible EU naval operation and urges States that have the capacity to do so to cooperate with the Transitional Federal Government of Somalia in the fight against piracy and armed robbery at sea. The UN Security Council also urges States and regional organizations to continue to take action to protect the World Food Programme (WFP) maritime convoys.

The EU has publically stated that it is very concerned by the recent proliferation of acts of piracy and armed robbery at sea against vessels off the coast of Somalia, and by the serious threat it poses:

- to the prompt, safe and effective delivery of humanitarian aid to Somalia,
- to international navigation and the safety of commercial maritime routes, and
- to fishing activities conducted in conformity with international law

In the deployment of its forces, the EU has reaffirmed its respect for the sovereignty, territorial integrity, political independence and unity of Somalia. The eradication of piracy in the region will only be achievable through the restoration of peace in Somalia. To this end, the EU acts within a comprehensive approach to achieve a lasting settlement of the Somali crisis, covering its political, security and humanitarian aspects.

7. CONCLUSION

The risk of being pirated is statistically small, but we can not overlook the impact that it has on stability and security in the region.

The ultimate solution to the problem is ashore, and will be hard to solve. The U.S. Navy and our international Coalition partners are committed to maintaining a presence in the region. We will continue to prevent destabilizing activities such as piracy in the maritime domain, while the larger international community works to improve the conditions ashore in Somalia.

I appreciate the opportunity to appear before the committee and stand ready to answer any questions the members of the committee may have.

Viktor Nikolsky
Captain, M/V FAINA
Indian Ocean
February 2009

Dear Captain Mark Genung and the crew of USS VELLA GULF,

On behalf of myself and the crew, I wish to show my sincerest appreciation for all the support VELLA GULF has shown us during our four months of captivity under the Somali pirates. Our liberation would not have been possible without your constant presence. It is difficult for me to express my feelings towards you and your crew. Our lives were spared because you were here to protect us. You gave us the strength to endure the hardest of times. We will keep VELLA GULF and her crew in our hearts and prayers forever. We wish you a safe journey home and good health for all your days. Thanks for everything you have done.

Your friend,

Viktor Nikolsky
Captain, M/V FAINA

Crew of M/V FAINA:

Viktor Nikolsky
Captain, M/V FAINA
Indian Ocean
February 2009

Dear Captain Charles Rodriguez and the crew of USNS CATAWBA,

On behalf of myself and the crew, I wish to show my sincerest appreciation for all the support CATAWBA has shown us during our four months of captivity under the Somali pirates. Our liberation would not have been possible without your constant presence. It is difficult for me to express my feelings towards you and your crew. Our lives were spared because you were here to protect us. You gave us the strength to endure the hardest of times. We will keep CATAWBA and her crew in our hearts and prayers forever. We wish you a safe journey home and good health for all your days. Thanks for everything you have done.

Your friend,

M/V FAINA IMO No 7419377 BELIZE CITY

Viktor Nikolsky
Captain, M/V FAINA

Crew of M/V FAINA:

In: Ocean Piracy
Editor: Jacob E. Nelson

ISBN: 978-1-60741-495-7

Chapter 3

TESTIMONY OF STEPHEN D. MULL BEFORE THE HOUSE COMMITTEE ON ARMED SERVICES ON COMBATING PIRACY ON THE HIGH SEAS

Chairman Skelton, Ranking Member McHugh, and Members of the Committee: Thank you for inviting me today to provide an overview of current U.S. efforts to suppress piracy. I am pleased to appear beside Admiral Gortney.

Over the past year the United States has noted with growing concern the emergence of piracy as a significant threat to international security and the global economy. American leadership in efforts to combat piracy off the Coast of Somalia is entirely consistent with our traditional interest in ensuring freedom of navigation and safety of the seas, which have long been cornerstones of U.S. foreign policy and which will be priorities for the new Administration and Secretary of State Clinton. Beyond ensuring the security of maritime trade and access to critical energy resources upon which our national and the global economies depend, collaboration with both traditional and non-traditional partners on counter-piracy in this region offers strategic opportunities to strengthen existing alliances and coalitions and to create new ones. Counter-piracy efforts could become mutually beneficial platforms for regional capacity-building programs and provide a non-controversial basis for security cooperation in the maritime domain with non-traditional partners such as China, Russia, and India.

Though U.S. ships have not been victimized by piracy attacks off the coast of Somalia, these attacks have disrupted U.S.-supported World Food Program transports delivering aid to some of the world's most vulnerable populations;

placed innocent mariners from countries across the globe in immediate danger; posed environmental threats as pirated ships may be damaged or run aground; and jeopardized commercial shipping interests.

The United States has developed a multifaceted strategy to suppress piracy that the Departments of State, Defense, Justice, Homeland Security, and Transportation are in the process of implementing. This strategy includes leading efforts to enhance existing international legal authorities to combat piracy; enhancing multilateral cooperation; collaborating closely with the international shipping industry; coordinating national and coalition military responses to piracy; and pursuing broader diplomatic and political approaches to the longer-term challenge of re-establishing a stable and secure environment in Somalia.

Though international law, as reflected in the Law of the Sea Convention, as well as the 1988 Convention for the Suppression of Unlawful Acts Against the Safety of Maritime Navigation and the United Nations Convention Against Transnational Organized Crime, already provides extensive international authority for the apprehension and prosecution of suspected pirates, the United States played a leadership role in securing the passage of United Nations Security Council resolutions 1846 and 1851, adopted late last year, that expanded international authorities to conduct counter-piracy operations off the coast of, and in, Somalia.

The United States is also pursuing bilateral arrangements with countries to ensure suspected pirates are appropriately charged and prosecuted. We are grateful for the leadership the Government of Kenya has shown in bringing to justice those persons engaged in piratical actions, including by concluding a Memorandum of Understanding with the United States for this purpose. We also hope to establish similar bilateral arrangements with other states to ensure that one country alone does not bear the burden of prosecution. Furthermore, we strongly encourage other states affected by an act of piracy to exercise their jurisdiction to charge and prosecute suspects in accordance with international law and any applicable national laws.

United Nations Security Council resolution 1851 also encouraged creation of an international mechanism to coordinate between states and organizations cooperating on combating piracy. Pursuant to this resolution, the United States hosted the first meeting of the Contact Group on Piracy off the Coast of Somalia (CGPCS) in New York on January 14. There, participating countries and organizations established four working groups to review and make recommendations on military and operational coordination and information sharing, judicial aspects of piracy, shipping best practices, and the diplomatic and public information aspects of piracy. The Contact Group, which currently numbers 34 participants, offers participation to nations and international organizations making tangible contributions to counter-piracy efforts, or any country significantly affected by piracy off the coast of Somalia, and may be expanded in the future.

With the support of the International Maritime Organization, the United States is leading the Contact Group's third working group, focused on strengthening shipping self-awareness and other capabilities. This working group met in London February 26 and 27 where a report on *Best Management Practices to Deter Piracy in the Gulf of Aden and off the Coast of Somalia* was presented by representatives of the International Chamber of Shipping on behalf of the shipping industry. We recognize the central importance of the shipping industry to counter-piracy efforts and look forward to continuing our collaboration.

The United States is also contributing to military efforts through Combined Task Force (CTF) 151, a multinational coalition with a specific mandate to conduct counter-piracy operations in the Gulf of Aden, Red Sea, and Indian Ocean. CTF-151 has joined other forces already operating in the region, notably EU NAVFOR-Operation. International counter-piracy military cooperation also extends to a number of countries – including Russia, China and India – that have deployed national missions to the area, and may grow in the future.

The United States recognizes there will be no long-term solution to piracy in the region unless progress is made in addressing the larger political, security and governance challenges facing Somalia, its government and its people. We also recognize that sustainable change in Somalia requires a political solution to conflict that is authored and implemented by Somalis themselves and not by outsiders. In this regard, the United States continues to support the UN-led Djibouti Peace Process, which has provided the mechanism for Somalis to make important political and security decisions in recent months, and work with a broad international group of donors to support the reconciliation process. The United States also remains committed to supporting the African Union Mission in Somalia (AMISOM) and Somalia security forces.

Over the past five months, the number of successful attacks has declined from an average of seven a month in October, November and December to only two a month in January and February. While we do not know with certainty the degree to which this decline is a direct result of our and/or our partners' efforts, we believe the unified response of the international community has been a contributing factor, and we plan to build on this success. The Contact Group will reconvene in two weeks at a meeting hosted by the Government of Egypt, where it will receive recommendations from the four working groups and consider the requests of other countries to join the group. We look forward to continuing these important discussions.

The area affected by piracy is of critical importance to the United States, both in economic and in political terms. We need to build upon the enhanced multilateral cooperation the international community has shown itself capable of bringing to bear against shared challenges to peace and security, both in the region and beyond.

We have developed an international consensus for better military, judicial and diplomatic coordination that provide a foundation for near-term regional benefits. International cooperation in support of counter-piracy can and should be expanded in support of security objectives that include building interoperability among forces in the region; extending cooperation in interdiction activities; improving international responses to humanitarian emergencies; and increasing our shared air and maritime domain awareness.

We will continue to explore these opportunities with our partners and will be working with them to identify appropriate areas for engagement.

Mr. Chairman, Ranking Member McHugh, and Members of the Committee: I want to thank you for this opportunity to provide an overview of our efforts. I am happy to answer any questions you may have.

In: Ocean Piracy
Editor: Jacob E. Nelson

ISBN: 978-1-60741-495-7

Chapter 4

TESTIMONY OF KARL WYCOFF BEFORE THE HOUSE COMMITTEE ON ARMED SERVICES ON COMBATING PIRACY ON THE HIGH SEAS

Mr. Chairman and Members of the Committee: thank you for affording me the privilege of discussing the relationship between the conditions in Somalia and the blight of piracy in the waters off its shores. Somalia piracy, *offshore*, is born out of instability and insecurity *on shore*. Consequently, a complete, long-term and permanent solution to the piracy problem off the coast of Somalia will require a multi-faceted strategy that leads to political and economic stability on the ground in Somalia and the establishment of basic security. To protect U.S. national interests, our immediate policy objectives in Somalia are to help Somalia regain political and economic stability, respond to the humanitarian needs of the Somali people, and eliminate the threat of terrorism.

Sustainable change in Somalia requires a comprehensive regional strategy and a political solution to conflict that is authored and implemented by Somalis themselves and not by outsiders. In this regard, we continue to support the United Nations (UN)-led Djibouti Peace Process, which has provided the mechanism for Somalis to make important political and security decisions in recent months. We also continue to work with a broad international group of donors to support the UN-led process, including the African Union and the regional Intergovernmental Authority on Development.

The Djibouti process has led to the establishment of a new unity government with a respected leader as President, Sheik Sharif Sheikh Ahmed, and a well-experienced Prime Minister, Omar Abdirashid Ali Sharmarke. The Prime Minister has now appointed a Cabinet. The new team represents a broad cross-section of

Somali clans and political opinions. The next step is for the unity government to foster deeper credibility with Somalis by establishing itself in Mogadishu, a process that has already begun, and to facilitate the delivery of services there and in surrounding regions. The United States worked with the other members of the UN Security Council Somalia Sanctions Committee to adopt resolution 1844 in November 2008, which empowers the Committee to designate spoilers of Somalia's reconciliation process for targeted sanctions.

While the recent political progress is encouraging, no political solution can be sustainable, even if widely supported, unless it is anchored by a robust security force capable of protecting the government and its activities. We encourage efforts by the international community to support the unity government as it stands up such a security force.

A good way to address African conflict or security issues is with African forces and expertise. Africans know and understand their terrain well, and have a paramount vested interest and stake in any outcome. In this regard, we continue to support the African Union Mission in Somalia (AMISOM) and are especially appreciative for the governments of Uganda and Burundi for sending soldiers to do the difficult work associated with peacekeeping in Somalia. We are currently funding the deployment of additional AMISOM battalions, which we hope will bring the total number of African Union forces on the ground in Somalia to over 5,000 within the next few months. Non-traditional donors, such as Gulf Arab states, have indicated a possible willingness to support AMISOM and the unity government's security force.

Mr. Chairman, it almost goes without saying that security must improve in order for displaced people to return home; without political stability the humanitarian situation will remain dire. We remain the largest bilateral donor of humanitarian assistance to Somalia. We hope the relocation of the unity government to Somalia and the stand-up of the joint security forces in Mogadishu will help improve security conditions at the community level and produce arrangements to facilitate humanitarian access so emergency assistance reaches those in need.

In: Ocean Piracy
Editor: Jacob E. Nelson
ISBN: 978-1-60741-495-7

Chapter 5

OCEAN PIRACY AND ITS IMPACT ON INSURANCE

Rawle O. King

SUMMARY

Many Members of 111th Congress are concerned about the sharp rise in pirate attacks in the strategic waterways in the Gulf of Aden off the East coast of Africa. The hijacking of a Saudi Arabia-owned oil tanker, *Sirius Star*, off the coast of Kenya on November 15, 2008, by pirates, and its release after a $3 million ransom payment on January 8, 2009, was another in a series of seizures and releases that have focused worldwide attention on economic and humanitarian threats posed by pirates to the global seafaring community and the smooth flow of international trade. Given the sharp increase in the number of pirate attacks, the cost of transporting cargo in international waters could rise dramatically because of the sharp increase in ocean marine insurance rates for ships transiting the Gulf of Aden. Commercial insurers, for example, could require a special "war risk" insurance premium costing an additional ten of thousands of dollars a day. These additional costs could adversely impact international trade during the current global economic slowdown.

In addition to proposals for military deterrence and diplomatic engagements, policymakers may elect to consider adjustments to the federal statute (Title XII of the Merchant Marine Act of 1936, as amended) that authorizes the federal government to underwrite marine war risk insurance in circumstances such as piracy. Title XII, administered by the U.S. Department of Transportation's Maritime Administration, authorizes the federal government to act as an insurer or reinsurer of last resort to facilitate waterborne commerce should private ocean marine insurance markets not be able to ensure that financial losses due to war risks (and piracy) will be largely covered.

Policymakers may also elect to maintain the status quo on this statutory authority. The property and casualty insurance industry policyholder surplus is calculated to be approximately $505 billion (as of June 2008). Vessel hull and war risk premiums in the U.S. market paid to insurers totaled approximately $350 million in 2007, and the total value of cargo insurance premiums paid in that year was approximately $833 million, according to industry data. Some may contend, as a result, that the insurance industry appears to be financially capable of handling U.S. exposure to the current piracy threat and that the existing policy "backstop" will be adequate.

INTRODUCTION

In the wake of the unprecedented number of pirate attacks on merchant ships off the Coast of East Africa in 2008, including the hijacking of a Saudi Arabia oil tanker (*Sirius Star*) carrying $100 million worth of crude, the global shipping industry and its insurance companies have called on governments to take immediate action to stop piracy in the Gulf of Aden and Indian Ocean.[1] Public attention has now focused on suspected Somali pirates who use sophisticated vessels and high-powered weapons to take control of large ocean-going ships carrying valuable cargoes. When pirates seize the ships they usually hold the crew hostage and demand money for the return of the crew, tanker and its contents (cargo). There are no reports of cruelty or destruction of vessels or the cargo. Piracy in the international waters off the East coast of Africa is arguably becoming viewed by the shippers, insurers, and pirates themselves as a well-established practice that functions in a business model that includes precise, well-established calculations of the amount to be paid as a ransom and professional assurances of the safety of crew, ship and cargo while negotiations proceed.

Shippers generally purchase ocean marine insurance to protect against a financial loss or injury to their crew, cargo and the ship itself. Still, pirates pose an economic threat to the global seafaring community and the smooth flow of international trade by commercial shipowners and operators. Also, the cost of transporting cargo could rise dramatically because of the sharp increase in commercial shipping insurance rates for ships transiting the area. By one estimate, due to piracy in the Gulf of Aden, the cost of insuring a container went from $900 in 2007 to $9,000 in the closing months of 2008.[2] These increases could trigger further rises in later phases of manufacturing and production.

THE CURRENT SITUATION

Piracy Events and Impacts

The Gulf of Aden was identified as an area of concern by Lloyd's Market Association (LMA) in May 2008.[3] The Gulf of Aden is considered a strategically important international waterway that carries a third of the world's crude oil. Over 20,000 vessels pass through this area each year. The Gulf of Aden lies between Yemen and Somalia and connects the Indian Ocean to the Red Sea and the Suez Canal. Other areas of the world that are viewed at risk for ocean piracy include Indonesia, Nigeria, Bangladesh and India.

Ocean marine insurers have urged shippers to stay at least 200 miles off the coast. On November 17, 2008, the *Sirius Star*, a Saudi-owned crude oil tanker, was seized in the Indian Ocean by suspected Somali pirates 450 nautical miles off the coast of Kenya in the Indian Ocean. The vessel remains anchored by the pirates near Harardhere, Somalia until its release in January 2009 with a $3 million ransom payment.[4]

The seizure of the *Star* was an unprecedented attack given its distance from shore (450 nautical miles) in the Indian Ocean and the size of its target (supertanker) compared to the majority of recent attacks. Shippers believe they can avoid the pirates by sailing farther offshore, but this means more time at sea and extra costs. As a result, ocean marine insurers are considering enlarging the war risk zone, a decision that would escalate the cost of shipping. Part of the higher cost would be the extra time and fuel consumed by going via the Cape of Good Hope rather than the Suez Canal. Also, insurers could require special "war risk" insurance costing tens of thousands of dollars more per day to cover travel across a much greater area of water.[5] Merchant shippers would also have to incur additional expenses to hire a security force to protect their vessels. One estimate of the added cost for security ranges as high as $60,000 per trip.[6]

On November 19, 2008, Pentagon officials released statistics showing that in 2008, there had been 95 reports of piracy attacks on merchant vessels in the Gulf of Aden, with 39 of these resulting in the capture of vessels.[7] The U.S. government has responded militarily to such piracy by sending four U.S. Navy warships from the Fifth Fleet in Bahrain to the Gulf of Aden off the coast of Somalia. Officials have also expressed an interest in working through the United Nations to encourage Somalia to curb piracy activities operating from its shores; an outcome that would be difficult to achieve since Somalia has no functioning government. The European Union sent a naval fleet to escort ships in the region. The U.S. warships have joined other warships from different countries such as Russia, China and Iran now patrolling the area.[8] According to Pentagon officials, many attacks were thwarted in December 2008 by the presence of military forces or by defensive measures taken by ship captains. U.S. military officials are encouraging merchants to sail with armed guards and to travel within lanes now patrolled by U.S. warships.

Insurance Industry Effects

Despite the increased threats and estimates of rising costs, the impact on the insurance industry appears negligible. Given the size of the property and casualty insurance industry's policyholder's surplus of about $505 billion, as of June 2008, and the relatively low total cost of vessel hull and war risk premiums of approximately $350 million and total cargo premiums written by U.S. marine insurance market in 2007 of $833 million, it appears that the insurance industry would be financially capable of handling U.S. exposures to acts of piracy in international waterborne commerce.

THE ECONOMIC COSTS AND CONSEQUENCES OF PIRACY

In May 2008, insurance underwriters at the Lloyds of London designated the Gulf of Aden a "war-risk" zone subject to a special insurance premium. London-based ocean marine insurers have raised rates for ships making the voyage through the Gulf of Aden and the Suez canal. These levels of increase can only be estimated because of the competitive nature of the ocean marine insurance business. One group of London insurance brokers and underwriters estimates extra premiums at $10,000 to $20,000 per trip through the Gulf.[9] U.S. rates, however, apparently have not changed. According to representatives of the American Institute of Marine Underwriters (AIMU), U.S. ocean marine insurers have not had to pay ransom for any act of piracy; therefore, they say, hull and cargo insurance rates for vessels leaving the United States remain the same.

The global shipping industry is most concerned about vessels that carry oil, chemicals, coal, iron ore, wheat and other commodities, because these vessels tend to be more vulnerable to pirate attacks than container vessels that carry manufactured goods. Container vessels are considered more difficult to seize by pirates because they ride higher in the water and are more difficult to board and seize from a small boat.

The increase in pirate attacks is occurring at a time when the shipping industry is expressing concerns about its financial health. One development is that the frequency of hiring dry bulk carriers, a key industry component, has decreased; the "hire" rates have dropped over 90% in the last six months.[10] (In some cases, the hire rate has dropped because the financial industry has stopped financing trade due to the global economic crisis.)[11] In addition, many ship owners and other key industry participants apparently face severe losses from the global financial market crisis. Some major dry bulk shippers lost money speculating on the market in shipping derivatives that offered potential for strong investment returns.[12] Shipping derivatives were developed to manage risk stemming from fluctuations in freight rates, vessel prices, interest rates, and foreign exchange rates, more effectively, in a cheaper and more flexible manner. Many shippers made derivative bets mistakenly on the direction of dry bulk rates during 2008.

With respect to the piracy issue, besides the *Sirius Star*, there are an estimated 14 other ships and their crews currently being held by pirates.[13] London-based shipping firms usually are, at times, prepared to pay ransom because the demanded sums are considered low, ranging from $500,000 to $2 million, compared with the value of the ships and its cargo. Such payments are reimbursed because the hull insurance policies issued in London explicitly cover the peril of piracy.[14] (Hull insurance forms used by American insurers generally exclude coverage for the peril of piracy.) Most of the 18 vessels, however, have cargo valued low enough that shippers likely will not pay the ransom demanded by the pirates; the ransom demanded exceeds the value of the cargo. One exception is a Ukrainian freighter currently being held by pirates, whose cargo includes military tanks, rocket-propelled grenades and antiaircraft guns. According to media reports, a deal has been reached for the ship's owners to pay an undisclosed ransom in exchange for the return of the ship.[15] In this case questions of public safety and threats of civil instability were considered along with financial calculations.

Basics of Marine Insurance

Marine insurance is coverage for goods in transit, and for the commercial vehicles that transport them, on water and on land. Marine insurance is divided into *inland marine* and *ocean marine* insurance. Inland marine insurance covers transportation-related or transportable property on land and air transportation as well as bridges, tunnels, and other modes. It is insurance for shipment that does not involve ocean transport.

American ocean marine insurance provides coverage for vessels and their cargo on the high seas, lakes or inland waterways. There are four basic types of ocean marine insurance:

- hull insurance that covers physical risk to the ship, like grounding or damage from heavy seas, collision, sinking, capsizing, being stranded, fire, piracy, and jettisoning cargo to save other property;
- cargo insurance that covers the goods transported in the ship;
- hull war risk insurance (including automatic termination and cancellation provisions in the event of war); and
- protection and indemnity (P&I) which covers liability involving the crew, docks and piers. Ship owners can purchase separate kidnap and ransom insurance for crew members.[16]

Hull Insurance

Hull insurance primarily covers physical damage to vessels (hull) and the machinery and equipment. The insurance also covers collision liability associated with damage to other vessels and their cargoes resulting from collision with the insured vessel. The hull insurance policy indemnifies the insured shipowner for these damages.

Most American shippers use the hull insurance form called *American Institute Hull Clauses* (AIHC), developed by the American Institute of Marine Underwriters, a trade association for marine insurers.[17] The AIHC is used primarily for oceangoing cargo and passenger vessels.

Another form, named the Taylor form, is often used for insuring vessels that traverse American rivers and coastal waters. In addition, it is customary for some insurance brokers to develop their own marine forms for submission to underwriters. This is possible because there is no standard form of marine insurance policy recognized by law in the United States.

American ship owners, operators, and merchants may also purchase marine insurance overseas, especially through the London market, which uses its own form. The London Institute hull form (known as the 1983 clauses or "Institute Time Clauses Hulls") explicitly covers loss or damage caused by piracy (page 58 of the form).[18] There is no exclusion. In order to provide uniformity, Great Britain codified its marine insurance law in the landmark *Marine Insurance Act of 1906*. This act established the Lloyd's form of policy as an example but is not a required policy form. The approach developed in Great Britain is to provide constant rules of interpretation so that there would be certainty of meaning and stability in ocean marine insurance transactions.

With respect to coverage for acts of piracy, it is instructive to note that the AIHC includes piracy as a named peril (on line 71) but excludes piracy (on line 245) as an insured peril in the event of war. Recognizing the war risk exclusion, U.S. shippers have the option of purchasing a separate war risk policy, called the *American Institute Hull War Risk and Strikes Clauses* which effectively covers the excluded war perils, including piracy.[19] However, even under the hull war risk insurance policy, the marine insurer retains the right to cancel the policy at any time. In the event the private insurer's war risk insurance is cancelled, the U.S. Department of Transportation's Maritime Administration's marine war risk insurance and reinsurance federal backstop automatically provides insurance and/or reinsurance to the ocean marine shipping industry (see "War Risk Insurance" discussion below).

Ocean Cargo Insurance

Ocean cargo insurance policies are written as separate coverage from hull insurance because merchants typically ship cargo via vessels owned by others. Ocean cargo insurance may be classified in two ways: policies issued to cover river and harbor cargo, and those issued to cover international trade that occurs on the oceans and seas. Cargo policies may also be classified by whether they are designed to cover a particular voyage, a specific time period, or a commodity such as grain, cotton, iron ore, or whether they are adapted to cover cargo general in its nature. Cargo policies may be issued for a single cargo risk (special or single risk cargo policies), and those that cover automatically all shipments of an insured (open or floating policies), subject to cancellation with 30 days' notice.

War Risk Insurance

Hull insurance usually does not cover the risk of a vessel sailing into a war zone, but such insurance can be purchased separately as "war risk insurance." War risk insurance is special coverage on cargo in transcontinental ships that protects against the risk of confiscation by a government in wartime. War risk insurance coverage protects, at an additional premium, against the danger of loss in a war zone. The war risk zones are established by the London-based Lloyd's Market Association's Joint War Committee (JWC), which has recently included the Gulf of Aden as a war risk area due to piracy.[20] (About a decade ago, the Malacca Straits were similarly designated a war risk area due to piracy.) The JWC represents the interests of underwriters writing war and related risks within the London ocean marine insurance market.

The U.S. Department of Transportation's Maritime Administration's (MARAD) marine war risk insurance program under Title XII, Merchant Marine Act, 1936, as amended, includes a provision of vessel war risk insurance, as follows.[21]

> The Secretary (of Transportation), with the approval of the President, and after such consultation with interested agencies of the Government as the President may require, may provide insurance and reinsurance against loss or damage by war risks in the manner and to the extent provided in this subchapter, whenever it appears to the Secretary that such insurance adequate for the needs of the water-borne commerce of the United States cannot be obtained on reasonable terms and conditions from companies authorized to do an insurance business in a State of the United States.[22]

During times of national emergency, at the request of the Department of Defense, the MARAD underwrites marine insurance risk insurance for DOD-chartered vessels during national emergency. Commercial shippers can obtain war risk insurance coverage from MARAD.

Protection and Indemnity Insurance

The hull insurance policy, even with the collision clause, does not protect the vessel owner against liability for damage to: cargo in the custody of the insured; injury to passengers, crew members, or laborers handling cargo; and damage to docks, piers, and other fixed objects. Vessel owners typically purchase a

Protection and Indemnity (P&I) marine insurance policy to cover these risks from shipowners' clubs that form to mutually insure these risks. In the 19th century, shipowners banded together in mutual underwriting clubs to insure liability risk amongst themselves. These clubs are still in existence today. Members of the clubs are generally levied an initial sum that is used to purchase reinsurance to cover their mutual liability risks. If a club experiences unfavorable losses, the members are assessed a supplementary premium. The club attempts to build up loss reserves.

OPTIONS FOR CONGRESS

Federal policy (Title XII of the Merchant Marine Act of 1936, as amended) authorizes the federal government to administer a maritime war risk insurance program that insures or reinsures, as a last resort, ocean-going commerce should private ocean marine insurance markets prove insufficient. Available statistics suggest that industry resources are adequate, given the property and casualty insurance industry surplus and the relatively low cost of insurance premiums. As a result, despite the increased activity of pirates, some may contend that Congress does not need to amend the existing federal insurance statutory construct. Others, however, may urge increased levels of oversight and investigation into the situation in an effort to ensure that international commerce remains stabilized, particularly at a time of global economic crisis.

End Notes

[1] *Piracy* may be defined as an act of violence at sea by passengers who mutiny and rioters who attack the ship from a boat launched from the shore.

[2] See *Maritime Reporter and Engineering News*, "American Officials Address Piracy," located at http://www4.marinelink.com/Story/American-Officials-Address-Piracy-213633.html.

[3] The Lloyd's Market Association (LMA) is the representative voice of the Lloyd's underwriting community.

[4] According to media reports, the *Sirius Star* is a Liberian-flagged crude tanker owned by Saudi Aramco, the Saudi Arabia's state oil company, and operated by Vela International, an Aramco subsidiary.

[5] John W. Miller, *The Wall Street Journal*, "Piracy Spurs Threats to Shipping Cost," November 19, 2008, p. A. 12.

[6] Ibid.

[7] See *Maritime Reporter and Engineering News*, "American Officials Address Piracy," located at http://www4.marinelink.com/Story/American-Officials-Address-Piracy-213633.html

[8] Thom Shanker, "U.S. Urges Merchant Ships to Try Steps to Foil Pirates," *New York Times*, November 20, 2008, p. 10.

[9] *Piracy Threat Hikes Insurance Premiums: Insurers to Raise Rates in High-Risk Areas After Piracy Heists Off Somali Coast*, November 20, 2008, located athttp://www.msnbc.msn.com/id

[10] Robert Wright, "Shipping in Crisis: Sector Must Navigate Rates Challenge," *Financial Times*, November 19, 2008, p. 18.

[11] Ibid.

[12] A derivative is a financial instrument whose price is dependent upon or derived from one or more underlying assets. The derivative itself is a contract between two or more parties. Its value is determined by fluctuations in the underlying asset. The most common underlying assets include stocks, bonds, commodities, currencies, interest rates and market indexes. Most derivatives are characterized by high leverage.

[13] *The Associate Press*, "Pirates Open Fire on U.S. Cruise Ship," December 2, 2008, located at http://www.msnbc.msn.com/id

[14] Robert F. Worth, "Pirates Seize Saudi Tanker off Kenya: Ship Called the Largest Ever Hijacked," *New York Times*, November 18, 2008, p. A. 6.

[15] Jeffrey Gettleman, Mediator Says Ransom Deal Has Been Reached for Pirated Ukrainian Freighter, The New York Times, December 1, 2008, p.

[16] In addition to hull, cargo, war risk and P&I insurance, other marine insurance polices are available to meet special needs. These policies include freight insurance, loss of charter hire insurance, builders risk insurance, and ship repairers legal liability policies. These policies are not at issue in the piracy threat.

[17] See *American Institute of Marine Underwriting*, "American Institute Hull Clauses," located at http://www.aimu.org./aimuforms/7.pdf.

[18] See *Institute Time Clauses (Hulls)*, located at http://alterisk.ru/download

[19] See *American Institute of Marine Underwriting*, "American Institute Hull War Risk and Strikes Clauses," located at http://www.aimu.org./aimuforms/87B-108.pdf.

[20] For information on the Joint War Committee, see, http://www.lmalloyds.com/AM/Template.cfm?Section=Joint_War1&Template=/TaggedPage/TaggedPageDisplay.cfm&TPLID=3&ContentID=3888.

[21] Merchant Marine Act, 1936, 46 U.S.C. App. 1282, 64 Stat. 773.

[22] *The White House*, "Presidential Memo on Marine War Risk Insurance Coverage," December 12, 2001, located at http://www.whitehouse.gov/news/releases/2001/12/print/20011214-9.html.

In: Ocean Piracy
Editor: Jacob E. Nelson

ISBN: 978-1-60741-495-7

Chapter 6

PIRACY OFF THE HORN OF AFRICA

Lauren Ploch, Christopher M. Blanchard, Ronald O'Rourke, R. Chuck Mason and Rawle O. King

SUMMARY

Pirate attacks in the waters off the Horn of Africa, including those on U.S.-flagged vessels, have brought new U.S. and international attention to the long-standing problem of piracy in the region. The International Maritime Bureau (IMB) recorded 111 attacks in the waters off the Horn of Africa in 2008, almost double the number in 2007. As of September 14, 2009, the U.S. State Department reported 156 attacks had occurred in those waters since January 2009, with 33 successful hijackings. Attacks remain concentrated in the Gulf of Aden between Yemen and the northern coast of Somalia and along Somalia's eastern coastline. However, in July 2009, the United Nations Secretary General warned that "as a result of the military presence in the region, pirates have employed more daring operational tactics, operating further seawards, towards the Seychelles, and using more sophisticated weaponry." Pirate attacks continue to threaten commercial shipping and relief shipments bound for East Africa and the Horn, amid a regional humanitarian crisis that experts are calling the worst since 1984.

The increase in pirate attacks off the Horn of Africa is directly linked to continuing insecurity and the absence of the rule of law in war-torn Somalia. The absence of a functioning government in Somalia remains the single greatest challenge to regional security and provides freedom of action for those engaged in piracy along the Somali coast. Some observers also have alleged that the absence of coastal security authorities in Somalia has allowed illegal international fishing and maritime dumping to occur in Somali waters, which in turn has undermined the economic prospects of some Somalis and may be providing economic or political motivation to some groups engaged in piracy. The apparent motive of many active Somali pirate groups is profit, and piracy has proven to be a lucrative activity for many thus far. Ransoms paid to Somali pirates and their supporters, estimated at over $30 million in 2008, may exacerbate ongoing fighting and further undermine security in the region.

The U.N. Security Council issued four resolutions (1816, 1838, 1846, and 1851) in 2008 to facilitate an international response to piracy off the Horn of Africa. At present, Resolution 1851 has authorized international naval forces to carry out anti-piracy operations in Somali territorial waters and ashore, with the consent of Somalia's Transitional Federal Government (TFG). Resolution 1872, adopted May 26, 2009, authorizes member states to participate in the training and equipping of the TFG security forces in accordance with Resolution 1772 (2007). In January 2009, a multilateral Contact Group on Piracy off the Coast of Somalia (CGPCS) was established to coordinate anti-piracy efforts. U.S., NATO, European Union, regional, and other naval forces are currently patrolling near Somalia in coordination with a U.S.-led Task Force.

Some members of the 111th Congress have expressed concern about the threat posed by piracy, and President Obama has stated that his Administration is resolved to halt the growth of piracy in the Horn of Africa region. The Obama Administration has outlined its policy response to the threat of piracy and pledged to continue working through interagency and multilateral coordination and enforcement mechanisms established during the Bush Administration. Most experts believe that the reestablishment of government authority in Somalia is the only guarantee that piracy will not persist or reemerge as a threat. The 111th Congress has explored a range of options to address both the threat posed by piracy as well as its underlying causes, and has sought to influence U.S. policy through oversight of U.S. military operations and diplomatic efforts and through defense and foreign assistance appropriations and authorizations.

Recent Developments

The summer months of 2009 saw a steep decline in the number of new pirate attacks in the waters off the Horn of Africa, after the blistering pace of attacks earlier in the year focused international attention on the challenges posed by piracy and insecurity in the region. Overall, the 156 pirate attacks in the Gulf of Aden and the waters off Somalia's eastern coast during the first nine months of 2009 exceeded the number of attacks—111—recorded in the region during all of 2008. Attacks remained concentrated in the Gulf of Aden, in spite of increased international maritime security efforts in those waters. The United Nations Secretary General warned that "as a result of the military presence in the region, pirates have employed more daring operational tactics, operating further seawards, towards the Seychelles, and using more sophisticated weaponry."[1] Data attributed to the International Maritime Bureau (IMB) stated that, as of late August 2009, approximately 104 non-U.S. crew members on 6 hijacked vessels remained in Somali captivity.[2]

The monsoon season weather credited with the summer decline in attacks began to improve in late August, and attacks have resumed. Warnings issued by the IMB's Piracy Reporting Center in August highlighted a rash of pirate attacks in the Bab el Mandeb strait and advised ships to transit at least 600 nautical miles from Somalia's eastern coast. The U.S. Department of Transportation Maritime Administration (MARAD) issued a September 2009 advisory warning U.S. vessels to "anticipate an increase in piracy attacks now through late December due to calmer weather favorable for small boat activity." The advisory further states that:

> Despite the increase in presence and effectiveness of naval forces in the region, as well as the effectiveness of defensive and protective measures, pirate activity has continued and a number of commercial and civilian ships have been successfully attacked and seized. There are indications that pirates in the area continue to adapt their techniques and procedures in order to achieve success in capturing vessels, both in the [Gulf of Aden] as well as in the open ocean off the east coast of Africa, particularly in the increased distances that they are able to operate effectively off the east coast of Somalia potentially utilizing mother ships. Naval vessels patrolling the [Maritime Security Patrol Area] provide a measure of deterrence through their presence, but this is limited due to the vast area of the [Gulf of Aden] and is even less effective in the open waters east of Somalia. Given the high volume of shipping in the region, the safety of all ships cannot be guaranteed due to the often long response times due to the considerable distances involved.[3]

The United States participated in meetings of the multilateral Contact Group on Piracy off the Coast of Somalia in March, May, and September 2009 (see "Contact Group on Piracy off the Coast of Somalia" below). At the September meeting, the Group approved a U.N. Multi-Donor Trust Fund to support the cost of prosecution and incarceration of piracy suspects by regional countries such as Kenya, which has taken responsibility for prosecuting most pirate suspects. The Contact Group's next meeting is scheduled for January 2010. Within the Group, U.S. officials have led the efforts of a working group seeking to improve awareness and implementation of self- defense best practices in the shipping and insurance industries. Since May 2009, the United States and several other governments have signed a Commitment to Best Management Practices to Avoid, Deter or Delay Acts of Piracy (the so-called "New York Declaration"), including popular ship registry countries such as Panama, Liberia, the Bahamas, and the Marshall Islands. Japan also has announced a $14 million contribution to an United Nations International Maritime Organization (IMO)[4] administered trust fund to support capacity building initiatives for regional signatories of the Djibouti Code of Conduct anti-piracy agreement (see "International Maritime Organization and the Djibouti Code of Conduct" below).

As international coordination of anti-piracy efforts has improved at sea and in the region in recent months, U.S. civilian and military officials have continued to stress the importance and difficulty of finding solutions to the problem of instability ashore in Somalia. To that end, the African Union (AU) has extended the mandate of their peacekeeping force in the country, known as the African Union Mission to Somalia (AMISOM), and the United Nations Security Council continues to consider proposals to send a U.N. force to Somalia to replace AMISOM. The U.N. Security council has pledged $72 million for AMISOM, and the United States has provided training, logistics support, and assistance worth over $135 million to AMISOM in the past two years.[5] AMISOM forces repeatedly have come under attack from Islamist groups opposed to the presence of foreign troops in Somalia, including the Al Qaeda influenced group known as *Al Shabaab* and a newer group, Hizbul Islam. A recent attack, a suicide truck bombing of an AMISOM base in Mogadishu on September 17, killed 21, including the AMISOM Deputy Force Commander and 16 other peacekeepers, and injured 40. Al Shabaab claims that the attack was committed in retaliation for a September 14 raid, alleged to have been conducted by U.S. special forces, in which Al Qaeda suspect Saleh Ali Saleh Nabhan reportedly was killed.

The U.S. government and international donors have expressed support for the new unity government formed between the TFG and the Alliance for the Reliberation of Somalia (ARS), which returned to Mogadishu in early 2009 with elected ARS leader Sharif Sheikh Ahmed as its president. Elements of the ARS based abroad, as well as groups and factions in Somalia, have vowed to continue fighting against the new government, and violence has surged since May. In response, the United Nations, the League of Arab States, the African Union, and the regional Intergovernmental Authority on Development (IGAD) issued a joint statement in June condemning the insurgents as a threat "not only to the country, but to the IGAD region and the international community."[6] The international Contact Group on Somalia continues to work on a multilateral basis to support Somali efforts to reach reconciliation agreements and implement the country's Transitional Federal Charter. An April 23 donors conference netted $213 million in pledges of support for AMISOM and TFG plans to support police and security forces.[7] On May 26, 2009, the United Nations Security Council unanimously adopted Resolution 1872, granting new authorization for members states to participate in the training and equipping of the TFG security forces in accordance with Resolution 1772 (2007) (see "United Nations Security Council" below).

The U.S. government, working through AMISOM partners, has provided TFG security forces with small arms and ammunition and funds to purchase weapons. This effort has raised concerns among some observers who claim that weapons provided to the TFG are being resold and benefiting insurgents.[8] According to U.S. officials, the United States has provided training to TFG security personnel and funds to the TFG to purchase weapons and ammunition. In mid-2009, the Administration arranged for "urgent" shipments of approximately 40 tons of small arms and ammunition to TFG forces in response to growing attacks from its enemies. As of June 2009, U.S. officials stated that the total value of the program was under $10 million.[9] In June 2009, State Department spokesman Ian Kelly said:

> At the request of [the TFG] government, the State Department has helped to provide weapons and ammunition on an urgent basis. This is to support the Transitional Federal Government's efforts to repel the onslaught of extremist forces, which are intent on destroying the Djibouti peace process and spoiling efforts to bring peace and stability to Somalia through political reconciliation. Any State Department assistance to the TFG underscores our longstanding policy of supporting the Djibouti peace process. This is also supported by the international community and follows on to our participation in International Contact Group meetings in Somalia.[10]

In April 2009, U.S. Secretary of State Hillary Clinton indicated that U.S. diplomats planned to engage with Somali Transitional Federal Government (TFG) officials and leaders from the semiautonomous region of Puntland (shaded in **Figure 1**) and the Eyl district to "press these leaders to take action against pirates operating from bases within their territories." Puntland authorities reportedly have taken some limited action in response (see "The Pirates" below).

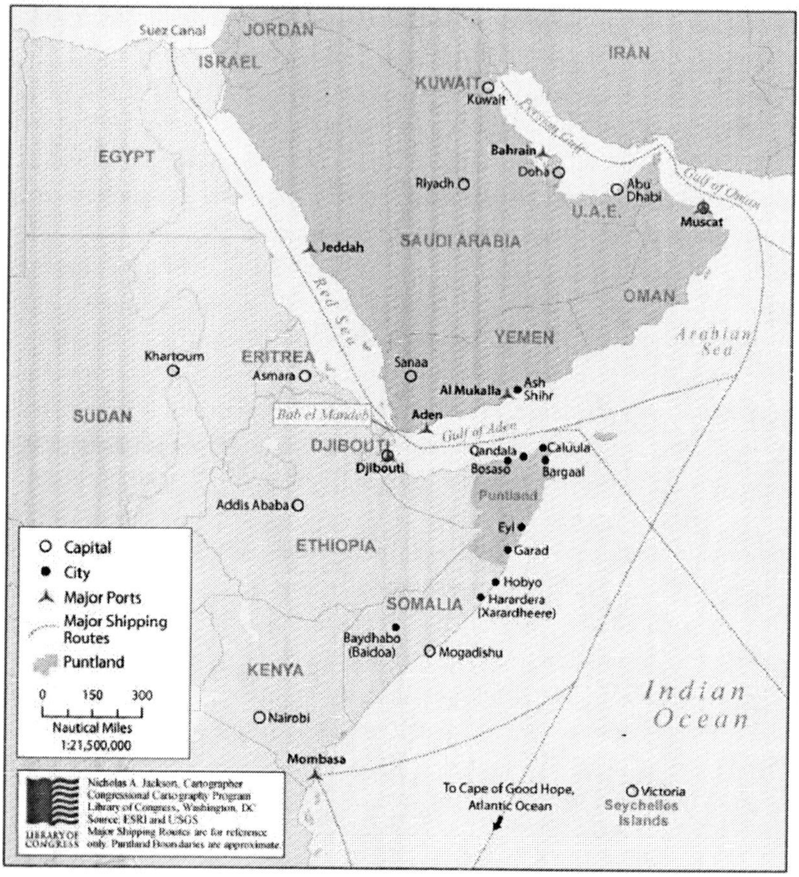

Source: Congressional Cartography Program, Library of Congress, adapted by CRS Graphics.

Figure 1 . The Horn of Africa, Surrounding Waters, and Key Locations

The Obama Administration requested $40 million in 2009 supplemental Peacekeeping Operations (PKO) funding to provide "non-lethal equipment, logistical support, and basing facilities for the African Union Mission to Somalia and to support Somali security sector reform." The Administration also sought authority to transfer up to $50 million in supplemental Contributions for International Peacekeeping Activities (CIPA) funding to the PKO account for Somalia, if necessary. For FY20 10, the Administration is requesting $67 million in PKO funding for Somalia, along with $2 million in Nonproliferation, Antiterrorism, Demining, and Related Programs funding for small arms and light weapons destruction programs (NADR-SALW) and $40,000 for International

Military Education and Training (IMET) programs. For more information about political developments in Somalia and U.S. policy, see CRS Report RL3391 1, *Somalia: Current Conditions and Prospects for a Lasting Peace*, by Ted Dagne.

On March 16, 2009, United Nations Secretary General Ban Ki-moon released his report to the Security Council required by Resolution 1846 on the security of international navigation off the coast of Somalia (S/2009/146). His next 1846 report is due in November 2009. The Secretary General reported to the Security Council on the Situation in Somalia in July 2009 and, as noted above, included warned of the increasing range of pirate attacks and provided an update on international anti-piracy efforts.[11]

BACKGROUND

Piracy has reemerged as a global security threat, most recently in the waters off the Horn of Africa, but also in West Africa, the waters off India, the South China Sea and the Strait of Malacca, and the Caribbean. Pirates tend to operate in regions with large coastal areas, high levels of commercial activity, small national naval forces, and weak regional security cooperation mechanisms. These characteristics facilitate other maritime security threats, including maritime terrorism, weapons and narcotics trafficking, illegal fishing and dumping, and human smuggling operations.

Worldwide rates of piracy began to increase in the early 1990s, peaking at roughly 350 to 450 reported attacks per year during the period 2000-2004, then declining by almost half by 2005. In 2007, almost half of the world's reported pirate attacks took place in African waters, mainly near Nigeria and Somalia. The number of attacks in Somali waters doubled in 2008, accounting for an estimated 40% of the 293 pirate attacks reported worldwide. [12] The recent increase in pirate attacks off Somalia is likely to cause the total number of worldwide pirate attacks to increase in 2009, but not necessarily back to the levels of 2000-2004. Nevertheless, high profile attacks in the Gulf of Aden and the west Indian Ocean have brought renewed international attention to the problem of piracy in waters off the Horn of Africa.

The U.S. National Maritime Security Strategy, issued in 2005, stated that the "safety and economic security of the United States depends upon the secure use of the world's oceans," and identified "well organized and well equipped" pirates and criminals as threats to international maritime security. The bombing of the *U.S.S. Cole* in 2000 in the Yemeni harbor of Aden and the bombing of the French oil tanker *MV Limburg* in 2002 illustrated the threat of potential maritime terrorism in the region. The United States, working with its international partners, established a combined naval task force in 2002 to meet the terrorism threat (Combined Task Force 150),[13] and increased bilateral military and security assistance to regional navies. However, prior to the establishment in 2008 of the new Combined Task Force 151 (see "Combined Task Force 151" below), the United States had not assigned any naval assets the sole task of performing anti-piracy operations in the Horn of Africa region.

Similarly, until 2008, the international community did not respond to the threat of piracy in the waters off of Somalia in a coordinated, dedicated manner. In December 2008, the European Union launched EU NAVFOR Operation ATALANTA, representing the first naval operation under the framework of the European Security and Defense Policy (ESDP). Similarly, NATO has launched a dedicated anti-piracy mission, Operation Ocean Shield, and other navies have deployed ships to provide security for vessels bearing their flags. The development of a collaborative regional response in East Africa in 2009 has mirrored regional reactions to the threat of piracy in the Strait of Malacca between Malaysia, Singapore and Indonesia, which are credited with having drastically reduced the instance of piracy in Southeast Asia since 2005 (see "International Maritime Organization and the Djibouti Code of Conduct" below). Eradicating piracy in the Horn of Africa region may prove to be a more daunting task. The vast areas of the western Indian Ocean and the Gulf of Aden where the pirates operate are remote, Somalia remains largely ungoverned, and regional states have relatively weak naval capabilities.

Piracy off the Horn of Africa: Profile

The Pirates

Several groups of pirates currently operate in Somali waters, according to reports from the United Nations Secretary General and an experts group convened by the Secretary General's Special Representative for Somalia in November 2008.[14] Organized predominantly along clan lines and based in distinct, remote port towns, the groups have varying capabilities and patterns of operation, making generalized responses more difficult. The two primary groups identified by Secretary General Ban Ki-moon in his March 2009 report were a pirate network based in the Puntland region district of Eyl and a pirate network based in the Mudug region district of Harardera (Xarardheere). The Secretary General and the Special Representative's experts group also report that smaller pirate groups also operate from the Somali ports of Bosaso, Qandala, Caluula, Bargaal, Hobyo, Mogadishu, and Garad.[15] The Secretary General has warned that some of the pirate groups "now rival established Somali authorities in terms of their military capabilities and resource bases." Other reports indicate that there may now be three distinct pirate groups, the Northern gang, based in Eyl; the Central gang, based in Hobyo; and the Southern gang, based in Harardera.[16] Pirate groups have operated from these remote communities, each heavily dependent on fishing, since the early 1990s.

The northern semi-autonomous region of Puntland (shaded in **Figure 1**) appears to be home to the most active and capable pirate networks, and some regional and local government officials there are alleged to have facilitated and profited from piracy prior to recent efforts by regional leaders to crack down on piracy-related corruption. In April 2009, Puntland security forces began to launch raids on pirate bases, and the region's courts have tried and convicted suspected pirates.[17] Local authorities also initiated *wa 'yigelin,* a "sensitization campaign" and have offered general amnesty to those that renounce piracy. Puntland's regional authorities have developed a basic coast guard, but accounts suggest that the equipment and capabilities of this small force remain very limited. Several of the pirate groups have adopted names to suggest that they are acting in a maritime security capacity, and some reports suggest that some of the pirates may have previously received training by Somalia's former navy and by foreign security firms and been given semi-official status to intercept foreign fishing vessels and extract fines. Today, the pirates are collectively referred to by Somalis as *burcad badeed* (sea bandits).[18] Nevertheless, piracy appears to have become an attractive pursuit for young men, creating potential legal complexities for regional and international governments seeking to try young pirate suspects for alleged crimes.

Motives

According to the final report of the experts group convened in November 2008 by U.N. Special Representative to Somalia Ahmedou Ould-Abdallah, "poverty, lack of employment, environmental hardship, pitifully low incomes, reduction of pastoralist and maritime resources due to drought and illegal fishing and a volatile security and political situation all contribute to the rise and continuance of piracy in Somalia."[19] While the profitability of piracy appears to be the primary motivating factor for most pirates, other observers argue that since conditions in Somalia make survival difficult for many and prosperity elusive for most, the relative risk of engagement in piracy seems diminished.[20]

Somali pirates interviewed by international media sources frequently link their piracy activities to trends such as illegal fishing and dumping in Somali waters that have emerged as the country has lost its ability to patrol its waters over time.[21] While these explanations may mask the opportunistic piracy of some, reports suggest that illegal fishing and dumping have disrupted Somalia's coastal economy. For example, a July 2005 report from the United Kingdom Department for International Development (DFID) estimated that Somalis lost $100 million to illegal tuna and shrimp fishing in the country's exclusive economic zone in 2003-2004.[22]

The international Contact Group on Piracy off the Coast of Somalia (CGPCS) (see "Contact Group on Piracy off the Coast of Somalia") stated at its inaugural meeting that "piracy is symptomatic of the overall situation in Somalia including the prevalence of illegal fishing and toxic waste dumping off the coast of Somalia, which adversely affects the Somali economy and marine environment."[23] The CGPCS also reaffirmed "its respect for Somalia's sovereignty, territorial integrity, and sovereign rights over natural resources" and underscored that the group's participants "ensure that their flagged vessels respect these rights."

Paradoxically, the regional fishing industry reportedly has been damaged significantly by the threat of piracy. According to some reports, tuna catches in the Indian Ocean fell 30% in 2008, in part because of fishing vessels' fears of piracy. This has had a major impact on countries like the Seychelles, which rely on the fishing industry for up to 40% of their earnings.[24]

The use of force by international naval patrols to apprehend or kill pirate suspects has raised the prospect that revenge may become a motivating factor for pirates whose associates are killed or captured. The April 14, 2009, attack on the U.S.-flagged *MV Liberty Sun* allegedly was carried out with the intention of damaging or sinking the ship and injuring or killing its crew in retaliation for the deaths of three Somali pirates during U.S. military efforts to secure the release of the detained captain of the *MV Maersk Alabama* days earlier (see "Threats to U.S. Flagged Vessels and the *MV Maersk Alabama* Incident" below).[25]

Tactics and Demands[26]

As noted above, some Somali pirate groups have developed sophisticated operational capabilities and have acquired weaponry, equipment, and funds that make them on par with or more effective than the local forces arrayed against them. The typical Somali pirate team is equipped with a variety of small arms, including AK-47 rifles and rocket propelled grenade (RPG) launchers. Many pirate teams use fishing skiffs powered with large outboard motors to give chase to larger, but slower moving tankers, cargo ships, yachts, cruise ships, barges, and tug boats. Local Somali fisherman reportedly are forced to support pirate activities in some cases, while in other cases, coastal Somalis lend their fishing boats, equipment, and navigational expertise to teams of would- be pirates from inland communities.

Somali pirates initially focused on attacking ships in the western Indian Ocean, off Somalia's eastern coast. When ships operating on that route shifted further out to sea, Somali pirates shifted their focus to the Gulf of Aden, where there is a concentration of merchant ships (an estimated 33,000 per year)[27] operating in a more constrained waterway that is relatively close to Somalia's northern shore. Most recently, now that international naval forces are patrolling the Gulf of Aden with some effectiveness, Somali pirates have shifted some of their focus back to the Indian Ocean, and are now able to operate hundreds of nautical miles from the Somali coastline, often with the support of so-called 'mother ships.' These 'mother ships' are larger fishing vessels often acquired or commandeered by acts of piracy, and tend to operate out of the Somali ports of Bosaso and Mogadishu and the Yemeni ports of Al Mukalla and Ash Shihr.

U.S. and international officials suspect that in some cases, Somali businessmen and international support networks provide pirate groups with financing and supplies in return for shares of ransom payments. The IMB has disputed claims that pirates receive intelligence support in order to target specific vessels, arguing that "the suggestion that vessels are targeted in advance using shore based intelligence is spurious.... Further, there is no information in the public domain that would enable pirates to precisely locate a targeted vessel at sea and then to mount a successful attack off the Horn of Africa."[28] The pirates refuel and purchase logistical supplies like fuel and engine parts in Yemen, according to U.S. naval officials.[29] According to the NATO Shipping Center, Somali pirates returning from raids in the Gulf of Aden often stop at the port of Caluula on the northeast tip of Somalia before proceeding to their safe havens on the Indian Ocean coast.[30]

One of the unique characteristics of Somali piracy has been the taking of hostages for ransom. In this sense, piracy off Somalia can be viewed as a form of maritime kidnapping. Unlike pirate attacks in Strait of Malacca or Nigeria, where ships are boarded either to take the vessel or its contents, pirates off the Horn of Africa routinely take the target vessel's crew hostage in return for ransom payments. This approach to piracy is possible because the pirates have a sanctuary on land in Somalia and in its territorial waters from which they can launch pirate attacks and conduct ransom negotiations. Pirates in other parts of the world are less likely to have such sanctuaries. This has presented maritime security forces with significant challenges to traditional engagement strategies and tactics.

According to reports, most vessels under attack have less than 15 to 30 minutes between the first sighting of the pirates and their boarding of the ship and taking of hostages. If a naval ship cannot arrive on scene within those 15 to 30 minutes, it will likely arrive too late to prevent the ship's capture. Naval combatant ships generally can steam at speeds of up to 30 knots (speeds of 20+ knots might be more likely), so unless a naval ship happens to be a few miles away when a commercial ship comes under attack, it won't arrive until after (perhaps long after) the 15- to 30-minute window has come and gone. The large area of water to be patrolled and the relatively small number of naval ships available means that the closest naval ship is often far too distant to arrive within that timeframe.

While pirate attacks may involve violence and the use of weaponry, most Somali pirate groups have not shown a willingness to wantonly harm captives taken in the course of their raids. Pirates in other parts of the world who engage in these types of attacks might be more likely to kill or seriously wound merchant ship crew members, since extracting ransom payments is not their objective. Negotiations for ransom involve the use of satellite telephones, third-party intermediaries in Somalia and abroad, and public relations efforts to influence interaction with property owners and foreign officials. Most navies have avoided rescue operations that could endanger the lives of hostages, preferring instead to engage in hostage negotiations or wait for shipping companies to negotiate ransom. According to reports, a rescue operation by French naval forces, designed to free a family held hostage onboard a small sailboat off the Somali coast, resulted in the death of the vessel's owner, a French citizen, during an exchange of fire between the pirates and naval personnel.[31]

Prior to the U.S. military resolution of the *MV Maersk Alabama* seizure and other French military operations, the most sensational cases of piracy to date had been resolved through the payment of large sums of money to different pirate syndicates.[32] The Ukrainian ship *MV Faina* was released for a reported $3.2 million ransom in February 2009 after being held for nearly 6 months by pirates based in Harardera (Xarardheere). The seizure of the ship, carrying T-72 tanks and a significant amount of ammunition and small arms, led several governments, including the United States, to dispatch naval forces to the region to monitor the ship and its cargo. The Saudi oil supertanker *MV Sirius Star* was released for a reported $3 million ransom to Eyl-based pirates in January 2009 following its seizure in November 2008. The hijacking of the *Sirius Star* illustrated the threat piracy may pose to international energy supplies as well as the capabilities of some Somali pirates to operate far out to sea against large vessels. Ransom payments are considered to be problematic by some observers because they encourage pirates to continue their attacks with the expectation that insurance and shipping companies will decide that ransoms are cost effective relative to the insured values of personnel and cargo (see "Threats to Commercial Shipping and Global Trade" below).

The use of force by international naval forces to apprehend pirates and to free hostages in 2009 has raised the prospect of an escalation in the pirates' use of force. As noted above, pirate leaders vowed to retaliate for the deaths of some of their operatives at the hands of U.S. and other international naval forces. However, to date few hostages have been harmed in pirate attacks. Nonetheless, the use of force against suspected pirate vessels also may be problematic because of the difficulty inherent in distinguishing a pirate mother ship from a legitimate commercial ship. According to reports, in November 2008, a ship from the Indian navy attacked what it thought was a pirate mother ship, only to discover, after the attack was conducted, that the targeted ship was an innocent Thai commercial trawler.

The effective use of force against pirate strongholds in coastal towns would likely require significant military planning and the investment of considerable resources in order to avoid or minimize civilian casualties. The number of naval ships that would be needed to completely halt piracy in the Gulf of Aden and the waters of Somalia's Eastern Coast is probably much larger than the force that has been operating there recently, approximately 30 combatant ships as of early September 2009. According to some estimates, as many as 60 might be required to fully suppress piracy in the Gulf of Aden alone. The adjoining area of concern in the Indian Ocean off Somalia's eastern coast, which has been measured at more than 1 million square miles, is much larger than the Gulf of Aden, so completely halting piracy in that area would likely also require an even larger number of ships.

Reports suggest that some pirates have invested ransom earnings in sophisticated weaponry and have fortified their operating bases against local authorities and potential international intervention. Some observers warn that international military operations to combat pirates ashore with force could undermine political reconciliation efforts aimed at reestablishing national governance in Somalia. (See "Oversight of U.S. Military Forces and U.S. Foreign Assistance" below.)

Piracy off the Horn of Africa: Impact

The strategic location of the Horn of Africa increases its importance for international security and commerce. The northern coastline of Somalia lies to the south of the Gulf of Aden, a key transit zone for ships passing to and from the

Red Sea and the increasingly active port of Djibouti. The U.S Department of Energy estimated that, as of 2006, as many as 3.3 million barrels of oil per day were transiting the Bab el Mandeb strait between the Gulf of Aden and the Red Sea.[33] The Indian Ocean waters off the southeast coast of Somalia are home to busy shipping lanes for trade between Asia and East Africa, as well as for ships making longer voyages around South Africa's Cape of Good Hope. Ship traffic to and from the Kenyan port of Mombasa is particularly vulnerable to security disruptions in the west Indian Ocean. The Maritime Administration testified in February 2009 that:

> On average, at least one U.S. commercial vessel transits the area each day. Many of these US-flag vessels carry Department of Defense cargo bound for Operations Iraqi and Enduring Freedom. U.S.-flag vessels transiting the region also carry humanitarian cargoes generated by U.S. AID or international organizations to the Horn of Africa, including Djibouti, Somalia and other countries in East Africa or South Asia.[34]

Threats to Commercial Shipping and Global Trade[35]

Somali piracy incurs economic costs in a number of ways, including ransom payments, damage to ships and cargoes, delays in delivering cargoes, increased maritime insurance rates, the costs of steps to harden merchant ships against attack, and costs for using naval forces for anti-piracy operations. The total economic costs of piracy, though significant in an absolute sense, are thought to be equivalent to only a very small fraction of the total value of worldwide shipborne commerce. In testimony on February 4, 2009, before the House Committee on Transportation and Infrastructure, Subcommittee on Coast Guard and Maritime Transportation, Peter Chalk, senior policy analyst at the Rand Corporation, stated that the overall annual cost of piracy to the maritime industry is estimated to be between $1 billion and $16 billion. Some of these costs are ultimately paid by the consumer.

In May 2008, insurance underwriters at Lloyds of London designated the Gulf of Aden a "war-risk" zone subject to a special insurance premium based on the advice of the U.K. insurance community's Joint War Committee. In response London-based ocean marine insurers have raised premium rates for ships making the voyage through the Gulf of Aden and the Suez Canal. These levels of increase can only be estimated because of the competitive nature of the ocean marine insurance business. One group of London insurance brokers and underwriters estimates extra premiums at $10,000 to $20,000 per trip through the Gulf.[36] U.S. rates, however, apparently have not changed. According to representatives of the

American Institute of Marine Underwriters (AIMU), U.S. ocean marine insurers have not had to pay ransom for any act of piracy; therefore, they say, hull and cargo insurance rates for vessels leaving the United States remain the same.

London-based shipping firms are usually prepared to pay ransom when the demanded sums are considered low, ranging from $500,000 to $2 million, compared with the value of the ships and cargo. Such payments are reimbursed because the hull insurance policies issued in London explicitly cover the peril of piracy.[37] (Hull insurance forms used by American insurers generally exclude coverage for the peril of piracy.) However, when the ransom demanded exceeds the value of the cargo, the shippers typically do not pay the ransom. Some firms have developed specific insurance products to address piracy-related ransom costs.[38]

Ship operators (and their governments) might judge that the costs of paying occasional ransoms are less than the costs of taking steps to prevent occasional hijackings such as rerouting or arming merchant ships. Some assert that payment of ransoms has tended to keep the level of violence associated with piracy off Somalia relatively low, and while individual ransom payments can be significant, the small percentage of ships operating in the area successfully attacked and captured lowers the overall risk in the eyes of some commercial entities. As such, the payment of occasional ransoms might be viewed by ship operators (and their governments) as a regrettable but tolerable cost of doing business, even if it encourages more piracy.

The increase in pirate attacks is occurring at a time when the shipping industry is showing vulnerabilities in its financial health. One development is that the frequency of hiring dry bulk carriers, a key industry component, has decreased; the "hire" rates dropped over 90% in late 2008.[39] (In some cases, the hire rate has dropped because the financial industry stopped financing some trade due to the global economic downturn.)[40] In addition, many ship owners and other key industry participants reportedly absorbed severe losses from the global financial crisis. Some major dry bulk shippers lost money speculating on the market in shipping derivatives that offered potential for strong investment returns.[41] Shipping derivatives were developed to manage risk stemming from fluctuations in freight rates, vessel prices, interest rates, and foreign exchange rates, more effectively, in a cheaper and more flexible manner. Many shippers made derivative bets mistakenly on the direction of dry bulk rates during 2008.

In addition to the generalized threat that piracy poses to the security of shipping lanes, the incidence of piracy has important second order effects on the costs, patterns, and benefits of regional and international shipping and trade. Egypt's Suez Canal serves as a vital shipping link between the Mediterranean Sea and Red Sea, and the revenue derived from ships transiting the Canal is an important source of funding for Egypt's government. Canal authorities report that shipping traffic and resulting revenue have declined over the last year, due both to decreased economic activity and the piracy threat to the Canal's approaches in the Gulf of Aden. Rerouting vessels to avoid the Gulf of Aden and other waters near the Horn of Africa adds additional transit days and fuel costs to shipping companies. The costs vary by type of ship and frequency of voyage, according to the U.S. Department of Transportation.[42]

Threats to Humanitarian Aid Deliveries

Piracy also threatens the delivery of vital humanitarian assistance to the Horn of Africa, much of which arrives by sea.[43] Almost 5 million Ethiopians required emergency humanitarian assistance in the first half of 2009, and the U.S. Agency for International Development (USAID) estimates that 6.2 million will require food aid in the latter half of the year. The United States provided over $600 million in humanitarian assistance to Ethiopia in FY2008, and has provided over $355 million to date in FY2009.[44] In neighboring Somalia, an estimated 3.2 million Somalis, approximately 43% of the population, required food aid in the latter half of 2008, and some 3.8 million are expected to require emergency assistance in 2009. U.S. humanitarian assistance to Somalia totaled $270 million in 2008 and over $150 million to date in FY2009.[45] The Obama Administration requested $200 million in FY2009 supplemental International Disaster Assistance (IDA) funding and $300 million in FY2009 supplemental P.L. 480, Title II humanitarian assistance, in part to address food and water shortages in Somalia, Ethiopia, and Sudan. For FY20 10, the Administration is requesting $40 million in P.L.480 funding for Ethiopia and $30 million for Sudan.

Food insecurity in the region, caused by drought and instability, has been heightened by high food and fuel prices in the region. Officials from the World Food Program (WFP), which ships tens of thousands of metric tons of food monthly to the Horn of Africa region, reports that it has become more expensive to ship assistance to Mogadishu, and that their ability to deliver relief is significantly hampered. A combination of rising costs, rising demand, and insufficient funding recently prompted WFP to announce that it would be closing feeding centers in Somalia. Canada, NATO, and European Union forces assumed WFP escort responsibilities in late 2008 (see "NATO: Operation Ocean Shield" and "European Union: Operation ATALANTA" below).[46]

Threats to U.S. Flagged Vessels and the MV Maersk Alabama Incident

The continuing threat of piracy to ongoing relief efforts and U.S.-flagged vessels was illustrated clearly in April 2009, when pirates hijacked the *MV Maersk Alabama* and attacked the *MV Liberty Sun*, both U.S.-flagged and crewed cargo vessels contracted by the WFP to deliver USAID food assistance off the southeast coast of Somalia. On April 8, 2009, Somali pirates seized the U.S.-flagged commercial shipping vessel *MV Maersk Alabama* approximately 250 nautical miles south east of the Somali town of Eyl. The *Maersk Alabama* had delivered food aid to the port of Djibouti and was en route to the port of Mombasa, Kenya, when it was seized by Somali pirates. Press reports suggested that the 20-member crew of U.S. citizens overtook their Somali captors some time after the ship was seized and attempted unsuccessfully to free the ship's captain, Vermont resident Richard Phillips.

In response, the United States Navy dispatched the *U.S.S. Bainbridge*,[47] an Arleigh Burke-class destroyer, and reconnaissance aircraft to the area in order to monitor the small craft where Captain Phillips was being held. Federal Bureau of Investigation personnel worked with naval personnel to conduct hostage negotiations for the captain's release. On April 11, after officials determined that Phillips' life was in immediate danger, U.S. special forces mounted a successful rescue operation with the authorization of President Barack Obama. Three pirates were killed by snipers in the U.S. rescue operation; a fourth, a young Somali named Abdiwali Abdiqadir Muse, has been indicted and has pled not guilty to piracy, conspiracy, hostage taking, and weapons charges before the United States District Court in the Southern District of New York.[48] Some analysts expressed concern that the rescue operation would trigger the use of increasingly violent tactics in future pirate attacks.

A leader of the pirate group based in the town of Eyl who held Phillips reportedly vowed revenge, telling reporters that, "this matter will lead to retaliation and we will hunt down particularly American citizens travelling our waters. Next time we get American citizens ... they [should] expect no mercy from us." An attack on a second U.S.-flagged vessel, the *MV Liberty Sun*, on April 14 appeared to be an attempt by pirates to make good on that threat. A pirate leader told reporters after the *Liberty Sun* attack that, "We were not after a ransom. We also assigned a team with special equipment to chase and destroy any ship flying the American flag in retaliation for the brutal killing of our friends."[49]

Potential Financing of Regional Conflict and Terrorism Concerns

The volatile Horn of Africa is home to several ongoing armed conflicts, and armed banditry is a common threat in much of the region. The small arms trade in the Horn and its potential to fuel instability remains a major concern to the international community. In spite of the longstanding United Nations arms embargo on Somalia established by Security Council Resolution 733 (1992), U.N. observers have reported "persistent violations" in recent years amid calls from the African Union and others for the lifting of the embargo to allow the armament of transitional government forces battling Islamist insurgents (see "United Nations Security Council" below). According to the Security Council Resolution 1851, "the lack of enforcement of the arms embargo ... has permitted ready access to the arms and ammunition used by the pirates and driven in part the phenomenal growth in piracy."

Observers have expressed apprehension that some of the revenue from ransoms paid for the release of ships and hostages may be used to finance an influx of more weapons to the area for pirates or others. According to some experts, some of the same boats used for pirate attacks are used to carry refugees and economic migrants from Somalia to Yemen, and many return carrying arms.[50] U.S. Navy officials have not found that fighters associated with *Al Shabaab* have financial ties to piracy at present, but the potential for personnel linkages may remain.[51] To the extent that ransom payments and new arms further empower criminal pirate groups, the challenge that such groups pose to local authorities at present and to reconstituted national authorities in the future could grow.

U.S. AND INTERNATIONAL POLICY RESPONSES

Piracy in the waters off the Horn of Africa is a symptom of the wider instability that has plagued Somalia and the region since the early 1990s. At present, the internationally recognized Transitional Federal Government (TFG) is working to form a functional unity government and to reconstitute national security and law enforcement entities. The Bush and Obama Administrations have supported reconciliation efforts in Somalia and have taken a leadership role in coordinating diplomatic and military responses to the threat of piracy in the region, in coordination with the United Nations Security Council. Funds pledged at the April 23 donors conference for Somalia in Brussels are intended in part to support the development of security forces by the TFG, and such forces, once developed, may improve local authorities' ability to act against pirates ashore. Some caution, however, that assistance provided to TFG forces may in some cases be transferred to the insurgent groups.[52]

To date, U.S. and international efforts to respond to the threat of piracy have taken on a multifaceted approach. In order to provide a short term response to the immediate threat to international navigation in the region's waters, the United Nations Security Council has authorized third party governments to conduct anti-piracy operations in Somali territorial waters and ashore, but only with authorization from and in coordination with the TFG. Among CTF- 151, the EU's Operation ATALANTA, NATO's Operation Ocean Shield, and other navies' "national escort" operations, approximately 30 combatant ships are currently patrolling in the region. Regional bodies such as the African Union, the Arab League, and ad hoc groupings such as the participants in the December 2008 International Conference on Piracy in Nairobi, Kenya, have held consultative meetings and issued policy statements condemning piracy in the region and providing guidance for the development of coordinated, collaborative regional responses.

U.S. Policy

The U.S. National Maritime Security Strategy, issued in 2005, stated that the "safety and economic security of the United States depends upon the secure use of the world's oceans," and identified "well organized and well equipped" pirates and criminals as threats to international maritime security. In June 2007, the Bush Administration adopted a Policy for the Repression of Piracy and other Criminal Acts of Violence at Sea that stated that it is the policy of the United States to "[c]ontinue to lead and support international efforts to repress piracy and other acts of violence against maritime navigation and urge other states to take decisive action both individually and through international efforts." In December 2008, the Bush Administration issued an implementation plan based on that policy to address piracy threats in the Horn of Africa region. The U.S. National Security Council (NSC) "*Countering Piracy off the Horn of Africa: Partnership and Action Plan*" set out the objective "to repress this piracy as effectively as possible in the interests of the global economy, freedom of navigation, Somalia, and the regional states."[53] In pursuit of that objective, the plan outlined three "lines of action" for U.S. policy:

> "1) prevent pirate attacks by reducing the vulnerability of the maritime domain to piracy; 2) disrupt acts of piracy consistent with international law and the rights and responsibilities of coastal and flag States; and 3) ensure that those who commit acts of piracy are held accountable for their actions by facilitating

the prosecution of suspected pirates by flag, victim and coastal States, and, in appropriate cases, the United States."

In support of the 2007 policy and 2008 plan, the Bush Administration formed an interagency Counter-Piracy Steering Group that "addresses the full spectrum of anti- and counter-piracy efforts, from piracy prevention to interruption and termination of acts of piracy, to ensure the accountability of pirates." The State Department and Defense Department are the co-leaders of the steering group and work with other U.S. government agencies, such as USAID and the Departments of Transportation, Homeland Security, Treasury, and Justice, to coordinate U.S. policies and engagement in the multilateral initiatives that have been developed since mid-2008. To date, the steering group has overseen efforts to implement elements of the December 2008 NSC *Action Plan*, which pledged U.S. support for the establishment of the international Contact Group on piracy (established January 2009, see "Contact Group on Piracy off the Coast of Somalia") and a regional counter-piracy coordination center (under development, see "International Maritime Organization and the Djibouti Code of Conduct").

The Obama Administration has endorsed the Bush Administration's overarching strategic approach with regard to the piracy threat, and over the course of 2009 Administration officials have outlined new implementation plans. In addition to providing expanded material assistance to the Somali Transitional Federal Government (TFG) in support of its efforts to provide security ashore, U.S. officials and military personnel have engaged with leaders and officials from the regions of Puntland to encourage them to take action against piracy and to improve coordination with international efforts. The United States remains a leading participant in the multilateral CGPCS, and has supported the "New York Declaration" initiative to establish benchmark best practices for governments, shipping companies, and insurance firms with regard to maritime security and piracy.[54]

The December 2008 *Plan* called for U.S. "bilateral assistance programs for judicial capacity building efforts" for regional states, and the Administration welcomed the September 2009 establishment of a trust fund to support regional prosecutions, but has not announced any U.S. contribution.[55] Comments from officials[56] suggest the Administration shares the view expressed in the Bush Administration Action Plan that U.S. anti-piracy efforts are intended "to be mutually supportive of longer-term initiatives aimed at establishing governance, rule of law, security, and economic development in Somalia."

United Nations Security Council

Resolution 1816 (June 2008) authorized states acting in cooperation with and with prior notification of the TFG to "enter the territorial waters of Somalia for the purpose of repressing acts of piracy and armed robbery at sea" and to "use, within the territorial waters of Somalia, in a manner consistent with action permitted on the high seas with respect to piracy under relevant international law, all necessary means to repress acts of piracy and armed robbery."[57] The initial authorization lasted for six months from June 2008. Resolution 1838, adopted in October 2008, called on states with military capabilities in the region to contribute to anti-piracy efforts and clarified the standing of the authorization contained in Resolution 1816 with respect to international law. [58]

At the request of the TFG, the mandate established in Resolution 1816 was extended for 12 months in December 2008 in Resolution 1 846.[59] In December 2008, Resolution 1851 expanded the mandate by authorizing states and regional organizations that are acting at the TFG's request to "undertake all necessary measures that are appropriate *in Somalia* [italics added] for the purpose of suppressing acts of piracy and armed robbery at sea."[60] Both resolutions require any authorized international measures to be undertaken in accordance with humanitarian and human rights laws. Other provisions of Resolution 1851 have guided developments since December 2008 and may inform future U.S or international initiatives (see "Contact Group on Piracy off the Coast of Somalia", "United Nations Office on Drugs and Crime", and "Oversight of U.S. Military Forces and U.S. Foreign Assistance" below).

Resolution 1846 authorized the provision of technical assistance to TFG personnel and forces "to enhance the capacity of these States to ensure coastal and maritime security" in accordance with procedures outlined in Resolution 1772.[61] Under paragraphs 11 and 12 of Resolution 1772, the supply of technical assistance to Somali "security sector institutions" is authorized provided that prior case-by-case notification is made to the U.N. arms embargo Committee for Somalia.[62] Resolution 1851 provides similar authorization to weapons and military equipment destined for the sole use of Member States and regional organizations undertaking authorized anti-piracy operations in Somali waters. The transfer of weaponry to Somali maritime security forces would require separate authorization from the Security Council. The African Union's Peace and Security Council and the TFG long requested that the broader U.N. arms embargo be amended or lifted in order to improve the capabilities of forces fighting Islamist insurgents. On May 26, 2009, the United Nations Security Council unanimously adopted Resolution 1872, granting new authorization for members states to participate in the training and equipping of the TFG security forces in accordance with Resolution 1772.

Contact Group on Piracy off the Coast of Somalia

Based on Resolution 1851, the Bush Administration led the formation of a multilateral Contact Group on Piracy off the Coast of Somalia (CGPCS) made up of 24 member governments and five regional and international organizations.[63] The Contact group held its first meeting in January 2009 and identified six tasks for itself: 1) improving operational and information support to counter-piracy operations, 2) establishing a counter-piracy coordination mechanism, 3) strengthening judicial frameworks for arrest, prosecution and detention of pirates, 4) strengthening commercial shipping self-awareness and other capabilities, 5) pursuing improved diplomatic and public information efforts, and 6) tracking financial flows related to piracy.[64] In support of these goals, four working groups make recommendations at periodic meetings of the Contact Group secretariat on relevant military/operational, judicial, diplomatic, and public information aspects of regional and international anti-piracy efforts. The goals of the working groups' efforts are to improve operational coordination, information sharing, and the effectiveness of legal enforcement activities among all regional and international actors combating piracy in the region.

The CGPCS met in March and May 2009 to begin planning a series of coordinated responses. The latest plenary meeting of the CGPCS was held in New York in September 2009, and its membership has grown to 45 member governments, seven regional organizations, and two observers.[65] The participants approved the creation of a U.N.-administered trust fund to help defray the costs assumed by regional states for the prosecution of piracy suspects. The next meeting is planned for January 2010.

Combined Task Force 151 and Other Navies' "National Escort Systems"

United States Naval Forces Central Command (NAVCENT) commands the Combined Maritime Forces operating in the Arabian/Persian Gulf, Gulf of Oman, Gulf of Aden, Red Sea, Arabian Sea, and Indian Ocean. In January 2009, the command established Combined Task Force 151 (CTF-151), with the sole mission of conducting anti-piracy operations in the Gulf of Aden and the waters off the Somali coast in the Indian Ocean. That role had previously been filled by CTF-150, which continues to perform counterterrorism and other maritime security operations as it has since 2001-2002. In August 2008, CTF 150 and partner forces agreed to the establishment of a Maritime Security Patrol Area (MSPA) in the Gulf of Aden to serve as a dedicated, more secure transit zone for merchant vessels. The MSPA has been credited in part with lowering the success rate of Somali pirates in the Gulf of Aden transit zone. Within the MSPA, eastbound and westbound Internationally Recommended Transit Corridors (IRTC) have been established "to de-conflict commercial transit traffic with Yemeni fishermen, provide a measure of traffic separation, and allow maritime forces to conduct deterrent operations in the [Gulf of Aden] with a greater degree of flexibility."[66] All U.S.-flagged vessels transiting the Gulf of Aden have been directed to plan their voyages using the IRTC.[67]

The list of countries participating in CTF-151 is fluid and consists of personnel and approximately two dozen ships from the United States, the United Kingdom, Canada, Denmark, France, Germany, Greece, Italy, the Netherlands, Pakistan, Saudi Arabia, Spain, South Korea, Turkey and Yemen, among others. Task force operations are coordinated from the NAVCENT command center in Bahrain. U.S. Coast Guard Law Enforcement Detachments (LEDETs) operate aboard CTF- 151 vessels and perform support and advisory missions during boarding operations and provide training to task force personnel on evidence procedures, maritime law, and related issues. As of August 2009, NAVCENT reported that, since January 2009, CTF-15 1 and other cooperating naval forces had "encountered 527 pirates; 282 of which were disarmed and released, 235 disarmed and turned over for prosecution, and 10 were killed."[68]

Other countries, most notably Russia, China, and India, have deployed naval forces to the region to participate in monitoring and anti-piracy "national escort system" operations. From an operational perspective, while these countries do not formally and fully coordinate their policies with CTF-151, there are ongoing communication efforts. A military coordination mechanism known as Shared Awareness and De-confliction (SHADE) coordinates the activities of coalition forces and Russia, China, India, and Japan. Naval observers and officials in the United States have noted the engagement of China with particular interest, as Chinese naval operations in the Horn of Africa region demonstrate the Chinese government's desire and ability to protect international shipping lanes far from China's shores.

NATO: Operation Ocean Shield

In October 2008, the North Atlantic Treaty Organization (NATO) deployed the first of two Standing NATO Maritime Groups to conduct anti-piracy operations in the Horn of Africa region. The first deployment, named Operation Allied Provider, served as a temporary protection force for World Food Program assistance shipments in the region. In December 2008, NATO ended Operation Allied Provider and transitioned WFP protection responsibilities to the European Union's new naval operation (see "European Union: Operation ATALANTA" below).

In March 2009, NATO launched a new anti-piracy mission, Operation Allied Protector, under the command of Standing NATO Maritime Group 1 (SNMG1). According to NATO, the forces participating in Operation Allied Protector acted to "deter, defend against and disrupt pirate activities." The Maritime Group was originally scheduled to perform temporary anti-piracy missions as it transited the Horn region en route to South East Asia and as it returned in June 2009.[69] In April 2009, NATO officials cancelled the planned SNMG1 visits to Singapore and Australia and extended the Operation Allied Protector mission until June 20, 2009. As of late March 2009, the following ships were participating in SNMG1 and Operation Allied Protector: *NRP Corte Real* (flagship, Portugal), *HMCS Winnipeg* (Canada), *HNLMS de Zeven Provinciën* (The Netherlands), *SPS Blas de Lezo* (Spain), and the *USS Halyburton* (United States).

In August 2009, NATO replaced Operation Allied Protector with a new anti-piracy mission, Operation Ocean Shield, under the command of Standing NATO Maritime Group 2 (SNMG2). Like its predecessor missions, Operation Ocean Shield has a primary responsibility to deter and respond to piracy. A new component of the mission is participation in capacity building efforts with regional governments. In relation to this new mission, the Group flagship has hosted maritime officials from the Puntland regional government and visited the Somali port of Bosaso in the northern province of Bari (see **Figure 2**, "Map of Somalia") for consultations with officials responsible for port security and maritime transportation.[70] As of August 2009, the following ships were participating in SNMG2 and Operation Ocean Shield: *HMS Cornwall* (flagship, United Kingdom), *HS Navarinon* (Greece), *ITS Libeccio* (Italy), *TCG Gediz* (Turkey), and *USS Laboon* (United States).

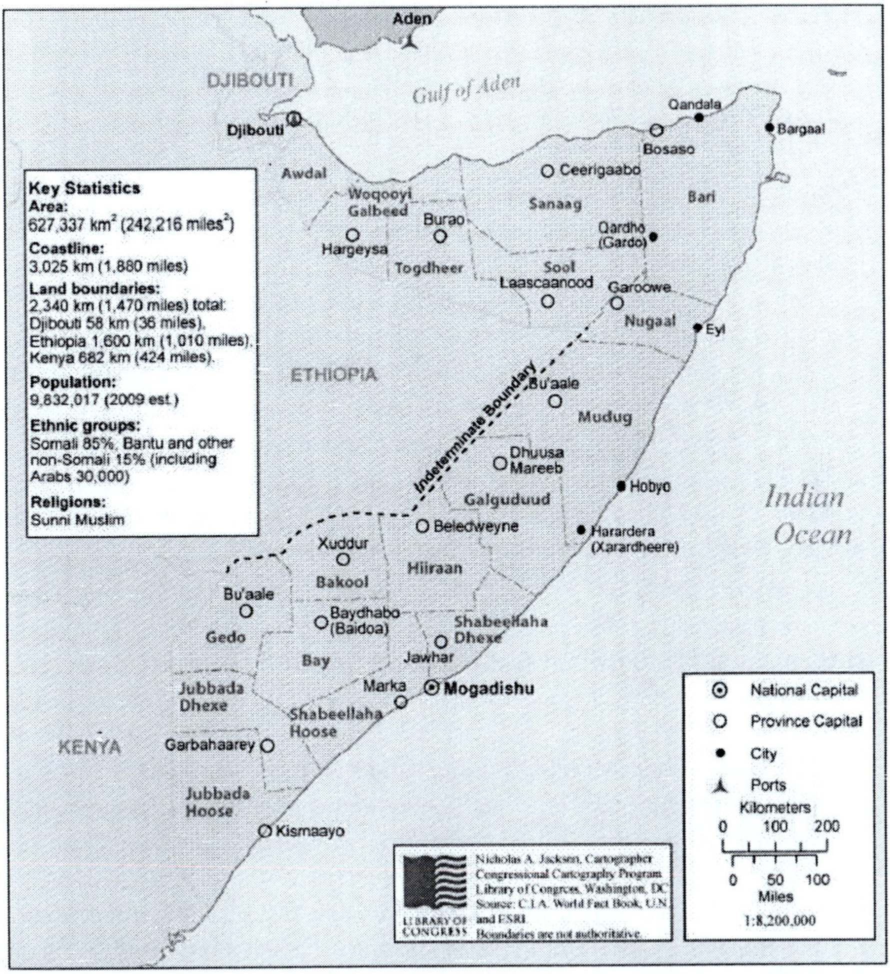

Source: Congressional Cartography Program, Library of Congress, adapted by CRS Graphics.

Figure 2: Somalia Map

European Union: Operation ATALANTA

In December 2008, the European Union launched EU NAVFOR Operation ATALANTA, its first naval operation under the framework of the European Security and Defense Policy (ESDP). Forces participating in Operation ATALANTA have been tasked with provide protection for WFP vessels and merchant vessels and are authorized to "employ the necessary measures, including the use of force, to deter, prevent and intervene in order to bring to an end acts of piracy and armed robbery which may be committed in the areas where they are present."[71] In June 2009, the European Council extended the mandate for Operation ATALANTA for one year from its original deadline of December 2009. According to the European Union, the operation will involve up to twenty ships and over 1,800 personnel over its full term. As of September 2009, the Netherlands, Spain, Germany, France, Greece, Italy, Sweden, Belgium, and Luxembourg have made permanent contributions of forces and personnel to the operation, and other EU member states support the operation's headquarters.[72] In coordination with the deployment, EU NAVFOR also has established an online center known as Maritime Security Center-Horn of Africa (MSC-HOA) for transiting ships to record their ships' movements voluntarily and to receive updated threat information.[73] Similar voluntary tracking and reporting services are provided by the United Kingdom Maritime Trade Operations office in Dubai and the U.S. Navy's Maritime Liaison Office in Bahrain.

International Maritime Organization and the Djibouti Code of Conduct

The International Maritime Organization (IMO)[74] has had an international anti-piracy program since the late 1990s and has successfully engaged on a multilateral basis in other regions to improve anti-piracy cooperation. At present, cooperative mechanisms for managing the security of the waters near the Horn of Africa are being developed as called for by the IMO[75] and as encouraged by Resolution 1851.[76] The IMO began sponsoring consultation meetings on piracy for the Horn of Africa region in 2005, which led to the development of a draft cooperative framework agreement in early 2008.

In January 2009, representatives of 17 regional governments met at an IMO-sponsored meeting in Djibouti and adopted a Code of Conduct concerning the Repression of Piracy and Armed Robbery against Ships in the western Indian Ocean and the Gulf of Aden.[77] As of late January 2009, nine regional governments[78] had signed the Code of Conduct, which remains open for signature by other parties. Three regional facilities—the Maritime Rescue Coordination Centre in Mombasa, Kenya, the Sub-Regional Coordination Centre in Dar es Salaam, Tanzania, and a regional maritime information center that is to be established in Sana'a, Yemen—are planned to support the information sharing components of the agreement. The parties also agreed to resolutions on technical cooperation and the establishment of a regional training center in Djibouti. In September 2009, Japan made an initial contribution of $14 million to a trust fund dedicated to supporting the IMO's Djibouti Code-related training and capacity building operations.

A similar cooperative framework developed by the IMO, the littoral states of the Strait of Malacca, and other Asian governments has been in force since 2006. Known as the Regional Cooperation Agreement on Combating Piracy and Armed Robbery against ships in Asia (ReCAAP),[79] the agreement established procedures for coordinating responses to piracy and sharing best practices among law enforcement and security personnel. The ReCAAP Information Sharing Center (ISC) in Singapore now serves as the principal clearinghouse for piracy reporting and response coordination.[80] These steps, taken in conjunction with other regional agreements between Malaysia, Indonesia and Singapore to coordinate anti-piracy patrols in the Straits of Malacca and surrounding waters, have been successful in reducing piracy in that region. The negotiation of the bilateral and multilateral initiatives in the Straits of Malacca region highlighted several issues that may be of interest to parties seeking to establish similar programs in the Horn of Africa region, namely the importance of addressing local concerns over sovereignty, territorial water rights, and the presence of foreign military forces in regional waters.

United Nations Office on Drugs and Crime: "Shipriders" and Capacity Building

Under the auspices of Resolution 1851 and in conjunction with the judicial working group of the (CGPCS), the United Nations Office on Drugs and Crime has launched a project to facilitate regional law enforcement participation in anti-piracy enforcement efforts off the coast of Somalia.[81] The program was encouraged in language included in Resolution 1851 and focuses on providing judicial capacity building assistance to regional states and facilitating so-called "shiprider" arrangements in which regional law enforcement personnel are seconded to international vessels to perform anti-piracy arrest and investigation functions. The United States has shiprider agreements with a number of Western Hemisphere governments to facilitate maritime security operations in waters of shared concern.

In general, shiprider arrangements are designed to address the logistical and legal challenges inherent in multilateral naval enforcement efforts in remote areas or where the capacity of regional governments does not allow for the provision of sufficient security. With regard to current operations in the Horn of Africa region, long transport times, limited military resources, legal limitations on the operations of military personnel, and complex differences in jurisdictional standards and requirements would complicate the arrest and prosecution by the varied non-regional forces operating under Resolution 1851. In order to help regional governments meet the added resource requirements that the arrest, detention, and prosecution of Somali pirate suspects would create, the UNODC plans to provide judicial capacity building assistance, in coordination with other donors. UNODC Executive Director Antonio Maria Costa testified before the House Foreign Affairs Subcommittee on International Organizations, Human Rights, and Oversight on the shiprider concept and proposed U.N. support in May 2009.[82]

Private Sector and Shipping Industry Responses

Private sector and shipping industry responses to the threat of piracy in the waters off the Horn of Africa have varied. In addition to altering financial decisions based on higher insurance costs, some accounts suggest that shipment navigation patterns have changed in response to the threat of piracy, with some vessels preferring to circumnavigate the southern Cape of Good Hope rather than risk attack in the Gulf of Aden. Crews also have developed a number of unique countermeasures and best practices in their attempts to ward off and resist pirate attacks. The use of water cannons, fire hoses, and passive sonic defenses has become more widespread, and industry surveys suggest that ships that operate at speeds above 15 knots[83] and that have higher freeboards[84] have proven less susceptible to pirate attack, thus far. Debates about the use of armed guards continue among shipping industry representatives, government officials, and observers worldwide (see "Options for Improving the Immediate Security of Merchant Ships").

The IMO and other bodies such as the International Chamber of Commerce International Maritime Bureau (ICC-IMB) have developed detailed guidance and recommendations for governments and commercial vessels seeking to prevent, deter, and respond to pirate attacks.[85] The IMB also has established a 24-hour piracy reporting center in Kuala Lumpur, Malaysia, which seeks to serve as the global, one-stop shop for piracy reporting and piracy threat information distribution for commercial vessels. The IMB also works with other regional information centers to collect and disseminate threat and situation reporting. For the Horn of Africa region, the IMB and European Union Maritime Security Center-Horn of Africa (MSCHOA) issue periodic "Industry Updates" detailing recent trends in pirate attacks and making recommendations to vessels transiting regional waters.[86]

ISSUES FOR CONGRESS AND POLICY OPTIONS

The risk of pirate attacks in the waters off the Horn of Africa is unlikely to disappear in the near term, and the United States government has identified piracy as a direct threat to U.S. national security interests. Policies developed by the Bush Administration to address Somali piracy have been revisited and enhanced by the Obama Administration in light of high profile attacks on U.S.- flagged vessels and crew members in April 2009.

Most defense analysts acknowledge that while the unprecedented level of naval patrols in the area—conducted by more than twenty nations—has deterred some attacks, the area is simply too vast to prevent all incidents. When the *MV Maersk Alabama* was attacked on April 8, 2009, the closest naval vessel, the *U.S.S. Bainbridge,* was approximately 300 nautical miles away. Similarly, the *U.S.S. Bainbridge* was only able to arrive on the scene of an aborted April 14 attack on the *MV Liberty Sun* a reported six hours after the attack ended. The continuing anti-piracy operations of international navies also comes at significant cost, as governments around the world weigh the budgetary impact of the current economic downturn and military requirements in other theaters of operation.

Like terrorism, acts of piracy in African waters pose a transnational security threat that emanates from areas plagued by conflict, weak governance, and economic insecurity. Continuing conflict in Somalia and Yemen illustrate the unstable regional context surrounding new anti-piracy operations. Regional security forces currently have limited maritime capability, and many governments have prioritized the development of their armies at the expense of navies or coast guards. That has changed to some extent in recent years, as international studies have highlighted the threat to local economies posed by illegal fishing, in addition to more traditional maritime security threats. Regional coordination and intelligence sharing also is weak.

The United States and its international partners have policy tools that have been used to address similarly complex security circumstances in other regions. However, ongoing U.S. and international security operations in environments such as Afghanistan, Pakistan, Iraq, and Colombia suggest that military intervention and foreign assistance require political consensus, political will, local partnership, and significant coordination in order to be successful. Maritime security efforts in the Persian Gulf, the Caribbean, the waters of West Africa, and the Strait of Malacca have had the same requirements. While short term results in containing other transnational threats have proven to be achievable, the long-term ability of international intervention to eliminate these threats is less certain in the absence of committed and capable regional and local actors.

Legislation in the 111th Congress

The 111th Congress has explored other options for protecting maritime traffic in the region. H.R. 3376, the U.S. Mariner and Vessel Protection Act of 2009, introduced in July by Representative Frank Lobiondo, aims to address the use of force and the right of self-defense of U.S. mariners against acts of piracy. Sec. 3505 of the House version of the National Defense Authorization Act for FY20 10, H.R. 2647, would require vessels carrying cargo for the Department of Defense in areas of high risk of piracy to be equipped with non-lethal defense measures to protect the vessel. H.R. 2647, Sec. 3506, would further require the Secretary of Defense to embark military personnel on board U.S.-flagged vessels carrying cargos owned by the U.S. government if a vessel is traveling in a high risk area and is determined by the Coast Guard to be at risk of being boarded by pirates. The Senate version of the bill did not include these measures.

Congress has also stressed that the U.S. government and others must address the piracy problem both at sea and on land. H.Rept. 111-166, accompanying H.R. 2647, expressed concern with continuing safe havens for Somali pirates, noting that "there does not appear to be a strategy for dealing with the organizations ashore in Somalia." S.Rept. 111-35, accompanying the FY20 10 National Defense Authorization Act, stressed the need for a "holistic approach," emphasizing the need for the commercial shipping industry to develop effective piracy countermeasures to protect its ships and crews.

Two resolutions passed by the House and Senate in April 2009 commended the crew of the *MV Maersk Alabama*, Captain Richard Phillips, and the U.S. military for its efforts in rescuing Captain Phillips and serving in anti-piracy missions (H.Res. 339 and S.Res. 108). The Senate resolution called on President Obama to "work with the international community and the transitional government of Somalia to develop a comprehensive strategy to address both the burgeoning problem of piracy and its root causes."

Oversight of U.S. Military Forces and U.S. Foreign Assistance

U.S. military engagement in the region is divided among two geographic combatant Commands. U.S. Central Command's area of responsibility (AOR) includes the waters of the Gulf of Aden and those off the eastern Somali coast, while the AOR of the new U.S. Africa Command (AFRICOM), which became fully operational in October 2008, encompasses the African continent.[87] To date, much of the U.S. military's anti-piracy response has been conducted at sea, by Central Command (CENTCOM). On land, AFRICOM provides security assistance to several regional maritime security forces, few of which have "blue water capacity." CENTCOM provides similar assistance to the Yemeni coast guard.

Oversight of U.S. Navy anti-piracy operations focuses on forces associated with CTF- 151 and with NATO's Operation Ocean Shield. Several U.S.-homeported Navy ships support the deployment of U.S. Navy ships operating on a continuous basis in the areas where Somali pirates are active. As such, the commitment of a single additional U.S. Navy ship to the area can affect the Navy's ability to perform missions in other parts of the world.

U.S. military operations in the region are not limited to anti-piracy efforts. The United States has conducted anti-terrorism activities in the Horn of Africa and in Yemen for over a decade, including the naval Combined Task Forces established as part of Operation Enduring Freedom. Djibouti has hosted a semi-permanent Forward Operating Site, known as the Combined Joint Task Force – Horn of Africa (CJTF-HOA) since 2003, with over 2,000 U.S. military personnel in residence. The command authority for CJTF-HOA, formerly under CENTCOM, has been transferred to AFRICOM. Its efforts initially focused primarily on countering violent extremism in the region, but the Task Force's activities have expanded in recent years to include a wide variety of activities aimed at building the capacity of regional militaries to respond to more general threats, such as natural disasters and armed conflict. CJTF-HOA personnel provide training to the region's security forces on counter-terrorism, maritime security, and peacekeeping.

As mentioned above, the United States conducts an array of maritime security assistance programs in East Africa and Yemen. In Kenya, for example, the United States provides maritime security assistance to both the Kenyan Navy and an array of agencies, including the Kenya Wildlife Service, revenue authority, and police, to address an array of threats, from smuggling and illegal fishing to terrorism. The U.S. also began support for a regional Maritime Center of Excellence in Mombasa in early 2009; courses at the Center are attended by participants from throughout East Africa. Several African countries, including Djibouti, Kenya, Tanzania, and Yemen, have received U.S. support for the installation of radar systems that provide enhanced maritime domain awareness. Congress expanded the Department of Defense's Section 1206 "train and equip" authority in FY2009 to include assistance for civilian maritime security forces. Several FY2009 Section 1206 programs aim support increased maritime capacity to address terrorist threats in the waters affected by Somali piracy, including programs for Djibouti, Yemen, Mozambique, Mauritius, Tanzania, and the Seychelles. In August 2009, AFRICOM and the government of the Seychelles announced an agreement with that will allow the U.S. military to operate P-3 Orion aircraft and unmanned aerial vehicles from the Seychelles in an effort to improve maritime surveillance in regional waters.[88]

U.N. Security Council Resolution 1851 "calls on Member States to assist the TFG, at its request and with notification to the Secretary-General, to strengthen its operational capacity to bring to justice those who are using Somali territory to plan, facilitate or undertake criminal acts of piracy and armed robbery at sea." The Obama Administration may seek to expand current assistance programs for regional and Somali actors subject to congressional appropriations and authorization and in accordance with United Nations Security Council resolutions. As noted above, the Obama Administration requested $40 million in 2009 supplemental Peacekeeping Operations (PKO) funding to provide "non-lethal equipment, logistical support, and basing facilities for the African Union Mission to Somalia and to support Somali security sector reform."[89] While those funds are likely to be directed toward improving Somali capacity to counter threats from insurgents and terrorists, to the extent that assistance improves the overall ability of government forces to operate effectively and assert security control, it may have positive implications for anti-piracy operations in the future. The Administration is requesting $67 million in FY20 10 PKO funding for Somalia.

Although some press reports in April 2009 quoted unnamed U.S. officials as stating that the U.S. military may consider launching military attacks against pirate strongholds, in testimony before the House Armed Services Committee in March 2009, Stephen Mull, then-Acting Undersecretary of State for International Security and Arms Control stated that although the United States supported the inclusion in Security Council Resolution 1851 of authorization for anti-piracy operations on land, there were, at that time "no plans to conduct counter-piracy operations on land."[90] Various parts of the U.S. government continue to encourage Somali figures in the Transitional Federal Government and in the region of Puntland to take action against pirate safe havens ashore. Overall, the Administration has signaled any major changes from the December 2008 National

Security Council *Partnership and Action Plan*, which states that the United States "will work with concerned governments and international organizations to disrupt and dismantle pirate bases to the fullest extent permitted by national law."

Piracy, Law Enforcement, and International Cooperation

Several United Nations instruments address the problem of piracy, including the Convention on the High Seas,[91] the Convention on the Law of the Sea (UNCLOS),[92] and the Convention for the Suppression of Unlawful Acts Against the Safety of Maritime Navigation (SUA Convention).[93] The United States is a signatory to the Convention on the High Seas and the SUA Convention, but not to UNCLOS. A "global diplomatic effort to regulate and write rules for all ocean areas, all uses of the seas and all of its resources" resulted in the convening of The Third United Nations Conference on the Sea in 1973 and the adoption of UNCLOS in 1982.[94] UNCLOS generally incorporates the rules of international law codified in the Convention on the High Seas, but also comprehensively addresses the use of other areas of the sea including, for example, the territorial seas, natural resources, and the seabed.

The Convention on the High Seas, to which the United States is a party, and UNCLOS both address piracy by stating that "[a]ll states shall cooperate to the fullest possible extent in the repression of piracy on the high seas or in any other place outside the jurisdiction of any State."[95] The term "piracy" is defined in UNCLOS (Article 101) as:

> (a) any illegal acts of violence or detention, or any act of depredation, committed for private ends by the crew or the passengers of a private ship or a private aircraft, and directed-
>
> (i) on the high seas, against another ship or aircraft, or against persons or property on board such ship or aircraft;
>
> (ii) against a ship, aircraft, persons or property in a place outside the jurisdiction of any State;
>
> (b) any act of voluntary participation in the operation of a ship or of an aircraft with knowledge of facts making it a pirate ship or aircraft;
>
> (c) any act of inciting or of intentionally facilitating an act described in subparagraph (a) or (b).[96]

Article 110 of UNCLOS authorizes warships to visit and/or inspect ships on the high seas that are suspected of engagement in piracy. Although the United

States is not party to UNCLOS, the Convention on the High Seas also authorizes the right of visitation/inspection of vessels suspected of being engaged in piracy.[97] States, under both the Convention on the High Seas and UNCLOS, are authorized to seize a pirate ship, or a ship taken by piracy and under the control of the pirates, and arrest the persons and seize the property on board.[98] The courts of the State whose forces carry out a seizure may decide the penalties to be imposed on the pirates.[99]

The SUA Convention further expands on the judicial treatment of pirates. Its main purpose is "to ensure that appropriate action is taken against persons committing unlawful acts against ships."[100] Unlawful acts include, but are not limited to, the seizure of ships; acts of violence against persons on board ships; and the placing of devices on board a ship which are likely to destroy or damage it.[101] The SUA Convention calls on parties to the agreement to make its enumerated offenses "punishable by appropriate penalties which take into account the grave nature of those offenses."[102] The United States criminalizes acts of piracy[103] and foreigners or U.S. citizens that commit acts of piracy are subject to imprisonment for life.[104] While it appears that U.S. law is sufficient to address the criminality of piracy, this may not be the case in other countries. Additionally, even with comprehensive criminal laws, the logistics related to the enforcement of the laws may be an impediment to their utilization.

Questions regarding legal jurisdiction, due process for detained pirate suspects, and the role of foreign military forces in anti-piracy law enforcement activities may complicate current U.S. and international operations against pirates in the Horn of Africa region. The most immediate legal concern associated with anti-piracy operations are jurisdictional questions that arise based on the location of pirate attacks and/or international naval interventions, the nationalities of crew members, and the countries of registry and/or ownership of any seized vessels.[105] Multiple governments may be able to assert legal jurisdiction depending on the specifics of the incident. But many governments lack sufficient laws and judicial capacity to effectively prosecute suspected pirates. The disposition of property and insurance claims for vessels involved in piracy also raises complex legal questions. A developing legal issue concerns the prosecution of juveniles participating in acts of piracy. Recent reports suggest that some of the Somali pirates are teenage minors,[106] and therefore could have a defense of infancy in certain jurisdictions that may assert jurisdiction over the offense.[107]

To date, some of these legal and law enforcement challenges have been addressed through the establishment of bilateral agreements by the United States, the United Kingdom, the European Union and others with governments in the Horn of Africa region, particularly with Kenya. Some agreements concluded to date define procedures for the detention, transfer, and prosecution of captured pirate suspects. For example, suspected pirates captured by U.S. military forces now may be transferred to Kenyan custody for prosecution according to the terms of a bilateral memorandum of understanding signed in January 2009. As of September 2009, 100 suspected pirates captured by warships from France, Germany, Italy, Spain, Sweden, the United Kingdom, and the United States are being prosecuted in Kenyan courts.[108] The United States has provided capacity building assistance to Kenya's Department of Public Prosecutions since 2005, and a resident legal advisor from the U.S. Department of Justice (DOJ) is providing the Kenyan government with assistance in piracy cases. DOJ has conducted several piracy workshops for prosecutors, police, and maritime security personnel. Other international donors have become increasingly engaged, and U.N. Office on Drugs and Crime (UNODC) is currently implementing a substantial capacity building program funded by the European Commission. As noted above (see "United Nations Office on Drugs and Crime: "Shipriders" and Capacity Building"), efforts also are underway to establish mechanisms for regional law enforcement personnel to serve as shipriders on coalition vessels and to expand the anti-piracy law enforcement and judicial capacities of neighboring states.

Options for Improving the Immediate Security of Merchant Ships

Risk Reduction and Best Practices

The U.S. Department of Transportation Maritime Administration (MARAD) issues detailed guidance to U.S. mariners transiting the waters off the Horn of Africa region to help ensure their safety and security.[109] Its latest guidance, issued September 9, 2009, includes instructions for U.S. flagged vessels seeking escort support from the U.S. Navy and Combined Maritime Forces participating in coalition naval security operations in the region.[110] As noted above, international bodies such as the International Maritime Organization[111] and the International Maritime Bureau[112] also have revised their recommendations for actions that merchant ships and their crews can take to reduce their risk of being attacked and captured.

These include measures that can be taken before and during pirate attacks. For example, rerouting ships, if possible, allows ships to avoid waters where Somali pirates are known to operate. This option can lengthen operating routes and increase shipping costs, but perhaps not as much as paying an occasional ransom. Recommendations suggest that transit of high-risk areas is not recommended at times of day when Somali pirates historically have been more likely to stage attacks, namely in early morning or dusk hours. In transit, effective watch procedures are recommended, since early detection of impending attacks increases the likelihood that avoidance and suppression measures will succeed. Higher ship operating speeds and evasive maneuvers have proven effective in many cases, as have denial systems such as barbed and razor wire and specialized electrical fences for ships. Crew preparation, training, and responses also are credited with reducing risks of successful pirate attacks.

Arming Merchant Ships[113]

Arming merchant ships can be done by either giving arms to the ship's crew, or by hiring armed security teams to ride on the ships. Some observers and industry representatives have advocated for these options as a means of ensuring that there is an immediate security presence aboard vessels to serve as a deterrent or to respond to pirate attacks. Supporters argue that the large geographic distances and limited responsiveness of international naval assets to piracy attacks makes the provision of on-ship security necessary. Others contend that the training of crew members to safely handle weapons does not pose an undue financial or practical burden to shipping companies. However, some merchant ship owners and operators are strongly averse to arming merchant ships, for practical and financial reasons.

U.S. government officials traditionally have expressed concern that merchant ships with armed crew members could pose security or terrorism risks visiting U.S. ports. As noted above, private or military gun battles with pirates can raise the overall level of violence associated with piracy off Somalia, which may increase risks to all merchant mariners on ships operating in that area. Since merchant ship crews are often not trained in the use of weapons, they might not be able to use them very effectively in fighting pirates. If ship crews try to defend themselves with firearms and fail, the pirates might be more likely to kill some of the crew members.

Even if used properly, lighter firearms might not be effective in countering pirates armed with heavier weapons, such as rocket-propelled grenades. Pirates with access to large amounts of money from prior ransom payments can acquire heavier weapons, so as to out-gun the merchant ships. In all cases, fire is a major safety concern, particularly on tanker ships, and gunfire could ignite vapors from the ship's cargo, or the cargo itself.

Financial concerns may also mitigate against arming merchant ships. Hiring armed security teams might be more expensive than paying occasional ransoms. Liability for fatal shootings aboard a ship can be a complex legal matter that can lead to expensive lawsuits. Since many ports restrict vessels from having weapons on board, commercial ships that often make calls at multiple ports along their operating routes could find it difficult to operate along certain routes. Reports suggest that private companies providing armed guards and shipping companies using armed security teams are grappling with these and other related issues in an effort to avoid legal trouble. Hugh Martin, general manager of security firm Hart Security UK has stated that "the amount of effort we put in to ensure we are legal is colossal."[114]

In mid-2009, the IMO Maritime Safety Committee released the following guidance:

> The MSC agreed that flag States should strongly discourage the carrying and use of firearms by seafarers for personal protection or for the protection of a ship... the use of unarmed security personnel is a matter for individual shipowners, companies, and ship operators to decide. The carriage of armed security personnel, or the use of military or law-enforcement officers (duly authorized by the Government of the flag State to carry firearms for the security of the ship) should be subject to flag State legislation and policies and is a matter for the flag State to authorize, in consultation with ship owners, companies and ship operators.[115]

International Traffic in Arms Regulations (ITAR)

The International Traffic in Arms Regulations (ITAR) may be an area of concern for ship owners desiring to arm their vessels in self-defense against acts of piracy. Section 38 of the Arms Export Control Act (ACEA)[116] authorizes the President to control the export and import of defense articles and defense services. The President, through Executive Order 11958, as amended, delegated the statutory authority to promulgate regulations with respect to exports of defense articles and defense services to the Secretary of State. The resulting regulations are known as the International Traffic in Arms Regulations.[117]

ITAR requires U.S. persons[118] to obtain a license in order to export or import items identified on the United States Munitions List.[119] As defined by regulation, the term "export" includes "sending or taking a defense article out of the United States[120] in any manner."[121] Objects covered by the term "defense article" are found on the United States Munitions List[122] and are classified into 21 separate categories. Categories I and III appear to be most relevant in a discussion regarding protection from acts of piracy because they include firearms (category I) and ammunition (category III) that could be used in the defense of a vessel. Based on the definitions of export and defense articles, a ship owner would be required to obtain a license for the temporary export of firearms and ammunition, or other covered armaments, for use in the defense of a vessel.

There is an exception to the licensing requirement under ITAR for the temporary export of not more than three non-automatic firearms and not more than 1,000 cartridges. To comply with this exception a U.S. person: (1) must declare the temporary export of the firearms and submit to an inspection by a customs officer; (2) must retain the firearms with the person (i.e., not mail the firearms to the destination); and (3) maintain the firearms for that person's exclusive use and not for reexport or transfer of ownership.[123] The regulation makes a distinction between U.S. persons and crew members of vessels, but how the distinction would affect the status of the vessel as an entity is unclear. [124] This exception may be an option available to owners as a way to arm their vessels, without obtaining an export license since the term "U.S. person" is defined to include a corporation, business association, and partnerships, as well as other entities. Additionally, it would appear that individual crew members would be able to temporarily export firearms under the exception. However, crew members utilizing privately owned weapons to defend corporate property could raise significant legal liability issues for both the individuals and the corporation.

The ITAR licensing requirement exception does not supersede prohibitions against exports to certain countries, including, but not limited to countries identified by the United Nations Security Council through a United Nations Arms Embargo.[125] Additionally, a license to export defense articles, or in the alternative obtaining an exemption from the licensing requirement, does not address or satisfy requirements of foreign countries that may exist with respect to operating a vessel in their territorial waters while carrying weapons. The vessel's owner is responsible for knowing and respecting the laws of the foreign country.

Convoys

Some observers argue that U.S. and international naval vessels should provide convoy protection services to ships transiting the Horn of Africa region, particularly the Gulf of Aden. Supporters argue that the direct participation of coalition or other naval assets in merchant ship convoys would eliminate the risks posed by unescorted travel through the Gulf of Aden or areas along the eastern coast of Somalia by cutting down the response times to attempted attacks. However, merchant ship operators may be reluctant to use a convoy system because it can require merchant ships to wait in a certain location for the next scheduled convoy to begin. The delays associated with this waiting can impose costs on ship operators that could be greater than the cost of paying an occasional ransom. The establishment and maintenance of a convoy system over the long term, in the absence of broader efforts to address the root causes of the piracy problem, could pose unacceptable costs for international navies.

Escorts by Navy Ships

As of September 2009, the current MARAD advisory indicates that U.S.-flagged vessels may contact U.S military headquarters in Bahrain to request escort services. Navy or Coast Guard vessels could escort U.S.-flagged commercial ships traveling in the Gulf of Aden, just as U.S. Navy vessels escorted U.S.-flagged ships (including reflagged Kuwaiti oil tankers) in the Persian Gulf in 1987-1988 (aka Operation Earnest Will) so as to protect them from potential Iranian attack during the Iran-Iraq war.

If Navy ships that are forward deployed to the Indian Ocean/Persian Gulf region were diverted from their current missions in that region to a mission of escorting U.S.-flagged commercial ships in the Gulf of Aden, the incremental financial cost (i.e., the additional dollar cost, above the costs that would be incurred if the ships continued performing their currently assigned missions in the Indian Ocean/Persian Gulf region) might be small. There would be an opportunity cost in terms of those ships not performing their currently assigned missions in the Indian Ocean/Persian Gulf region. Such missions can include engagement activities aimed at building or reinforcing U.S. partnerships with other countries in the region, humanitarian assistance and disaster-response (HADR) operations, intelligence, surveillance, and reconnaissance (ISR) operations, counterterrorism operations, deterrence of regional aggression, and crisis response and containment. Policymakers might need to weigh the potential advantages of escorting U.S.-flagged commercial ships in the Gulf Aden against the potential disadvantages of reduced Navy capacity for performing other missions in the Indian Ocean/Persian Gulf region.

If Navy ships that are forward deployed to other regions, such as the Mediterranean or the Western Pacific, were diverted from their current missions in those regions to a mission of escorting U.S.-flagged commercial ships in the Gulf of Aden, the incremental financial cost could be larger due to the need to expend additional fuel to transit to and from the Gulf of Aden region. Even so, the incremental financial cost might be relatively small as a fraction of annual Navy costs for ship operations. There would again be an opportunity cost in terms of those ships not performing their currently assigned missions in the regions from which they were diverted, which again can include things such as engagement activities, HADR operations, ISR operations, counterterrorism operations, deterrence of regional aggression, and crisis response and containment. Policymakers might again need to weigh the potential advantages of escorting U.S.- flagged commercial ships in the Gulf Aden against the potential disadvantages of reduced Navy capacity for performing missions in areas such as the Mediterranean or Western Pacific.

Armed Security Details of U.S. Military Personnel

An alternative to having U.S. Navy (or Coast Guard) ships escort U.S.-flagged commercial ships would be to provide a small security detail of armed U.S. military personnel to each U.S.-flagged ship for the duration of its transit through the Gulf of Aden. The detail would board each U.S.- flagged ship at the start of its transit through the high-risk zone and depart the ship at the end of its transit through the high-risk zone. One person who has suggested this alternative—a retired U.S. Navy vice admiral—asserted that "A few well-armed teams aboard a few ships could accomplish this mission" of protecting U.S.-flagged commercial ships traveling through the area."[126] An August 2009 news report states that France has placed military personnel aboard tuna fishing boats in the Indian Ocean and Belgium has offered eight-person military teams at a cost of $162,000 per week.[127] Some U.S. corporate officers have argued that military teams should protect U.S.-flagged in order to avoid "regulatory shortfalls, liability concerns, and international reluctance to permit armed merchant vessels into their ports."[128] Section 3506 of the House- passed version of H.R. 2647, the FY20 10 Defense Authorization act, would require the Secretary of Defense to embark military personnel on board U.S.-flagged vessels carrying cargos owned by the U.S. government if a vessel is traveling in a high risk area and is determined by the Coast Guard to be at risk of being boarded by pirates. The Senate version of the bill did not include these measures.

Maritime War Risk Insurance and Implications of "Armed Crews"

Federal law (Title XII of the Merchant Marine Act of 1936, as amended) authorizes the federal government to administer a maritime war risk insurance program that insures or reinsures, as a last resort, ocean-going commerce should private ocean marine insurance markets prove insufficient. Available statistics suggest that the insurance industry's financial resources are adequate, given policyholder surplus levels, and there is ample supply of coverage for oceangoing vessels, albeit at an elevated insurance premium level.[129] As a result, despite the dramatic increase in piracy off the coast of Somalia and increased premiums for sending a cargo shipment through the Gulf of Aden, some may contend that Congress does not need to amend the existing federal insurance statutory construct.

Others have urged arming ship crew as a risk mitigation option; Congress might consider steps to allow armed crews on some ships or support the use of military personnel in response to the current wave of piracy. Ocean marine insurers are conflicted on the "armed crew" issue. Some insurers believe traditional negotiations after an act of piracy—that lead to prompt formula-based ransom payments and a professional understanding between ship owners and the pirates about not damaging the ship or cargo in exchange for expedited payments—are the best approach to minimizing the cost of ocean marine transportation in piracy zones. Acts of piracy are actually declining in other areas although piracy still poses a threat to shipping and trade. Some might contend that arming ship crews would introduce new forms of armed conflict and increase the risks to cargo, vessels, and crew associated with piracy. Still other insurers would support increased levels of oversight and investigation into the piracy situation in an effort to ensure that international commerce remains stabilized, particularly at a time of global economic crisis.

Toward a Long-Term Solution: "Piracy is a Problem that Starts Ashore"[130]

Some Members of Congress have called on the Administration to develop a "comprehensive approach" to Somalia that responds to the threat of piracy in the context of a broader initiative to stabilize the country and support transitional government institutions. Some U.S. officials support a similar approach. In January 2009, Dr. Jun Bando, Maritime Security Coordinator and U.S. AFRICOM Liaison for the U.S. Department of State Bureau of African Affairs argued that "a durable solution for ending piracy in the Horn of Africa will require improving security, stability, rule of law, and economic opportunity in Somalia, as well as solidifying political progress by forming a unity government and advancing the peace process."[131]

Beginning in January, the Obama Administration signaled its intention to continue working with U.S. partners in the Contact Group on Somalia and the Contact Group on Piracy off the Coast of Somalia toward those goals. In response to recent attacks on U.S.-flagged and -crewed vessels, a more robust anti-piracy policy has been developed, and official statements indicate that the Administration intends to proceed on a multi-track basis by building regional capacity, supporting multilateral anti-piracy initiatives, and improving coordination in the U.S. interagency.[132] The Administration's interagency Counter-Piracy Steering Group continues to lead the efforts of over 75 bureaus, offices, and embassies engaged in anti-piracy operations. The State and Defense Departments lead the Steering Group and the Departments of Transportation (U.S. Maritime Administration [MARAD]), Justice, Homeland Security, Treasury, and USAID are members. Enhanced U.S. assistance to the Somali Transitional Federal Government and engagement with regional Somali representatives also aims to strengthen the ability and willingness of Somalis to secure regions where pirates currently enjoy safe havens.

> **"Ultimately, piracy is a problem that starts ashore and requires an international solution ashore. We made this clear at the offset of our efforts. We cannot guarantee safety in this vast region."**
>
> Vice Admiral William Gortney
> Commander, U.S. Naval Forces Central Command
> Testimony before the House Armed Services Committee, March 5, 2009

In the short term, the international community has responded to the threat of piracy in the waters off the Horn of Africa with multinational naval patrols, diplomatic coordination efforts, and enhanced private security efforts by members of the commercial shipping industry. In the longer term, U.S. officials and international experts believe that addressing the threat of piracy will require the strengthening of regional security capabilities, improved intelligence gathering and sharing, more effective and capable law enforcement, and enhanced multilateral coordination, both at sea and on land. By all accounts, pirates will likely continue to find sanctuary in Somalia until basic governance and security conditions there improve, a prospect threatened by ongoing conflict.

End Notes

[1] Report of the Secretary-General on the situation in Somalia, S/2009/3 73, July 20, 2009.
[2] Mike Cohen, "Ship Hijackings Off Somalia May Resume After Monsoon," *Bloomberg*, August 26, 2009.
[3] U.S. Department of Transportation Maritime Administration Advisory #: 2009-07, Gulf of Aden, Red Sea and Indian Ocean Transit, September 9, 2009.
[4] The International Maritime Organization is a United Nations agency with over 168 member governments. Based in the United Kingdom, its members develop regulations for international shipping related to safety, the environment, and maritime security. It also serves as a global coordinating body for legal issues, technical co-operation, and maritime security including anti-piracy efforts. For more information, see: http://www.imo.org/.
[5] Remarks by U.S. Ambassador Susan E. Rice, U.S. Permanent Representative to the United Nations, Security Council Debate On Somalia, July 9, 2009.
[6] U.N. Political Office for Somalia, "Joint Statement on the Assassination of Somali Security Minister," June 18, 2009.
[7] Agence Europe, "EU/SOMALIA: With $213 million promised, international community surpasses expectations," April 24, 2009.
[8] See claims made by Peter Pham cited in Fawzia Sheikh, "As Washington Crafts Somalia Review, Arms Deal Draws Criticism," *Inside the Pentagon*, Vol. 25, No. 34, August 27, 2009.

[9] A June 2009 background briefing from an unnamed senior U.S. State Department official described the effort as providing "small arms and limited munitions," explaining that the United States has provided "funds for the purchase of weapons; and we have also asked the two units that are there, particularly the Ugandans, to provide weapons to the TFG, and we have backfilled the Ugandans for what they have provided to the TFG government." U.S. State Department, "Background Briefing on U.S. Assistance to the Somalia Transitional Federal Government," Washington, DC, June 26, 2009.

[10] U.S. State Department Daily Press Briefing, Washington, DC, June 25, 2009.

[11] Report of the Secretary-General on the situation in Somalia, S/2009/3 73, July 20, 2009.

[12] Much of the statistical information on pirate attacks found in this report has been provided by the International Maritime Bureau, a division of the International Chamber of Commerce.

[13] See the U.S. Navy's website for CTF 150, available at: http://www.cusnc.navy.mil/command/ctf150.html.

[14] Report of the Secretary-General pursuant to Security Council Resolution 1846 (2008), S/2009/146, March 16, 2009; and, International Expert Group on Piracy off the Somali Coast, Final Report: Workshop commissioned by the Special Representative of the Secretary General of the UN to Somalia Ambassador Ahmedou Ould-Abdallah, November 10-12, 2008, Nairobi, Kenya.

[15] The Special Representative's experts group report identified the following specific pirate group leaders (clan, location in parentheses): Isse Mahmuud and Leelkase (Darood, Eyl), Omar Mahmuud (Darood, Garad), and the Habargedir (Hawiye, Hobiya, Harardera, and Mogadishu).

[16] International Crisis Group, *Somalia: The Problem with Puntland*, Africa Briefing No. 64, August 12, 2009.

[17] *All Africa*, "Anti-Piracy Campaign Begins Today in Puntland," April 24, 2009; and, *All Africa*, "Puntland Nabs 15 Pirate Suspects, Seizes 5 Boats," May 18, 2009.

[18] Ibid.

[19] International Expert Group on Piracy off the Somali Coast, Final Report: Workshop commissioned by the Special Representative of the Secretary General of the UN to Somalia Ambassador Ahmedou Ould-Abdallah, November 10-12, 2008, Nairobi, Kenya.

[20] The dire economic and security situation in Somalia is illustrated by the continuing outflow of refugees and migrants to neighboring countries. The U.N. High Commissioner for Refugees estimates that as many as 50,000 people, predominantly Somalis, crossed the Gulf of Aden to Yemen in 2008. The deaths of hundreds of migrants in a boat accident off the northern Somali coast in April 2009 illustrate a pattern of similar accidents which continues. "More Somali Migrants Drown off Yemeni Coast," UN IRIN, March 1, 2009.

[21] The U.N. experts group noted the tendency of pirates to characterize their actions as an alternative livelihood or as retribution for illegal international activities in Somali waters: "The pirates also firmly believe that they have every right and entitlement to attack illegal fishing vessels operating in their territorial waters as their fishing resources are being pillaged daily by international shipping vessels from Asia and Europe." International Expert Group on Piracy off the Somali Coast, Final Report, p. 15.

[22] DFID, "Review of Impacts of Illegal, Unreported and Unregulated Fishing on Developing Countries," July 2005.

[23] Statement of the Contact Group on Piracy off the Coast of Somalia, New York, January 14, 2009.

[24] "Somali Piracy 'Reduces Tuna Haul,'" *BBC*, January 22, 2009.

[25] An alleged pirate commander named Abdi Garad told reporters, "This attack was the first against our prime target. We intended to destroy this American-flagged ship and the crew on board but unfortunately they narrowly escaped us. The aim of this attack was totally different. We were not after a ransom. We also assigned a team with special equipment to chase and destroy any ship flying the American flag in retaliation for the brutal killing of our friends." *Agence France Presse*, "Pirates stage rocket attack on US freighter," April 14, 2009.

[26] The U.S. government has provided mariners with descriptions of common pirate tactics and instructions for response. See, for example, U.S. Department of Transportation Maritime

Administration, "Somali Pirate Tactics," December 2008. Available at http://www.marad.dot.gov/documents/HOA_Somali%20Pirate%20Tactics_15DEC2008.pdf.

[27] Assistant Secretary Andrew J. Shapiro, U.S. State Department, Bureau of Political-Military Affairs, "Taking Diplomatic Action Against Piracy," Remarks to the Global Maritime Information Sharing Symposium, National Defense University, Washington, D.C., September 16, 2009.

[28] International Chamber of Commerce- International Maritime Bureau, "Shipping Industry dismisses reports of targeted Somali pirate attacks," May 15, 2009.

[29] Comments by Admiral Mark Fitzgerald in "Work with Yemen Government on Somali Piracy: U.S. Admiral," *Reuters*, March 9, 2009.

[30] Report of the UN Secretary General, S/2009/146, paragraph 6, page 2.

[31] Others onboard were rescued safely.

[32] The French military also has reportedly undertaken a number of raid and rescue operations since April 2008 to free its citizens held aboard seized ships.

[33] U.S. Department of Energy, Energy Information Administration, Country Analysis Brief: World Oil Transit Chokepoints, January 2008.

[34] U.S. Department of Transportation, Maritime Administration, Statement of Acting Deputy Administrator James Caponti before the Sub-committee on Coast Guard and Maritime transportation of the Committee on Transportation and Infrastructure, United States House of Representatives, on International Piracy, February 4, 2009, p. 3.

[35] For more information about the commercial impact of piracy, see CRS Report R40081, *Ocean Piracy and Its Impact on Insurance*, by Rawle O. King.

[36] *Piracy Threat Hikes Insurance Premiums: Insurers to Raise Rates in High-Risk Areas After Piracy Heists Off Somali Coast*, November 20, 2008, located at http://www.msnbc.msn.com/id

[37] Robert F. Worth, "Pirates Seize Saudi Tanker off Kenya: Ship Called the Largest Ever Hijacked," *New York Times*, November 18, 2008, p. A. 6.

[38] Stuart Collins, "Insurers increase war rates for several high-risk areas" *Business Insurance*, Volume 43; Number 31, September 7, 2009.

[39] Robert Wright, "Shipping in Crisis: Sector Must Navigate Rates Challenge," *Financial Times*, November 19, 2008, p. 18.

[40] Ibid.

[41] A derivative is a financial instrument whose price is dependent upon or derived from one or more underlying assets. The derivative itself is a contract between two or more parties. Its value is determined by fluctuations in the underlying asset. The most common underlying assets include stocks, bonds, commodities, currencies, interest rates, and market indexes.

[42] For example, circumnavigation rather than transiting the Gulf of Aden/Suez Canal increases the annual operating cost of an oil tanker "by reducing the delivery capacity for the ship from about six round-trip voyages to five voyages, or a drop of about 26%. The additional fuel cost of traveling via the Cape of Good Hope is about $3.5 million annually." U.S. Department of Transportation Maritime Administration, Economic Impact of Piracy in the Gulf of Aden on Global Trade, December 2008.

[43] Food insecurity in the region is also exacerbated by banditry, roadblocks, inter-clan fighting, and attacks on aid workers.

[44] USAID, Complex Emergency – Ethiopia, Situation Report #11, September 17, 2009.

[45] USAID, Complex Emergency – Somalia, Situation Report #8, August 25, 2009.

[46] Christian Fraser, "On Patrol with the Pirate Hunters," BBC, November 21, 2008.

[47] The *U.S.S. Bainbridge* is named for Captain William Bainbridge, the commander of the *U.S.S. Philadelphia* who was held in captivity in the Barbary state of Tripoli from 1803 to 1805 after the *Philadelphia* ran aground in Tripoli harbor during anti-piracy operations. The captivity of Bainbridge and his crew significantly escalated the military confrontation between the United States and the Barbary pirates, whose threats to U.S. vessels in the Mediterranean were a key factor in the early development of the United States Navy. For more information, see http://www.bainbridge.navy.mil/sitepages/history.aspx.

[48] See complaint U.S. v. Abduwali Abdukhadir Muse, 09-MG-1012, U.S. District Court, Southern District of New York, April 21, 2009; and Alexandra Marks, "Teen Somali to be Tried as Adult," *Christian Science Monitor*, April 21, 2009.

[49] *Agence France Presse*, "Pirates stage rocket attack on US freighter," April 14, 2009.

[50] International Crisis Group, *Somalia: The Trouble with Puntland,* Africa Briefing No. 64, August 12, 2009.

[51] Vice Admiral William Gortney, the commander of U.S. Naval Forces Central Command told the House Armed Services Committee on March 5, 2009, that "We look very, very carefully for a linkage between piracy and terrorism or any kind of ideology and we do not see it. It would be a significant game changer should that linkage occur. But we have not seen it. We watch very carefully for it."

[52] Jeffrey Gettleman, "In Somalia, a Leader Is Raising Hopes for Stability," *New York Times*, September 17, 2009.

[53] U.S. National Security Council, "Countering Piracy off the Horn of Africa: Partnership and Action Plan," December 2008. Available at: http://www.marad.dot.gov/documents/Countering_Piracy_Off_The_Horn_of_Africa _Partnership__Action_Plan.pdf.

[54] U.S. State Department, "The United States Signs "New York Declaration," Washington, DC, September 9, 2009.

[55] Donna Hopkins, Plans and Policy Team Leader, U.S. State Department Bureau of Political-Military Affairs, Office of Plans, Policy, and Analysis, "Safeguarding the Seaways: Counter-Piracy Contact Group Meets in New York," *Dipnote*, September 17, 2009. Available at: http://blogs

[56] Secretary of State Hillary Clinton, "Announcement of Counter-Piracy Initiatives," Washington, DC, April 15, 2009.

[57] S/Res/1816 (2008) available at: http://www.un.org/Docs/sc/unsc_resolutions08.htm.

[58] S/Res/1838 (2008) available at: http://www.un.org/Docs/sc/unsc_resolutions08.htm.

[59] S/Res/1846 (2008) available at: http://www.un.org/Docs/sc/unsc_resolutions08.htm.

[60] S/Res/1851 (2008) available at: http://www.un.org/Docs/sc/unsc_resolutions08.htm.

[61] S/Res/1772 (2007) available at: http://www.un.org/Docs/sc/unsc_resolutions07.htm.

[62] For more information, see the Committee web page at: http://www.un.org/sc/committees/751/.

[63] Resolution 1851 "encourages all States and regional organizations fighting piracy and armed robbery at sea off the coast of Somalia to establish an international cooperation mechanism to act as a common point of contact between and among states, regional and international organizations on all aspects of combating piracy and armed robbery at sea off Somalia's coast."

[64] Statement of Contact Group on Piracy off the Coast of Somalia, New York, January 14, 2009.

[65] U.S. State Department Bureau of Political-Military Affairs, "Contact Group on Piracy off the Coast of Somalia: List of Participants, Fourth Plenary Meeting," New York, NY, September 10, 2009.

[66] U.S. Department of Transportation, Maritime Administration Advisory # 2009-07, Gulf of Aden, Red Sea, and Indian Ocean Transit, September 9, 2009.

[67] Ibid.

[68] Ibid.

[69] The task force is scheduled to visit Karachi, Pakistan, Singapore, and Perth, Australia, before returning to the Horn of Africa Region.

[70] NATO Allied Maritime Component Command, "NATO works with Somali officials," August 14, 2009. Available at: http://www.manw.nato.int/page_operation_ocean_shield.aspx.

[71] European Union Council Secretariat, "Fact Sheet: EU naval operation against piracy (EU NAVFOR Somalia -Operation ATALANTA)," EU NAVFOR/04, March 2009.

[72] EU NAVFOR Somalia - Operation ATALANTA, "Fact Sheet: EU Naval Operation Against Piracy," September 17,2009.

[73] Information on the Maritime Security Center-Horn of Africa (MSC-HOA) is available at: http://www.mschoa.eu/Default.aspx.

[74] The International Maritime Organization is a United Nations agency with over 168 member governments. Based in the United Kingdom, its members develop regulations for international shipping related to safety, the environment, and maritime security. It also serves as a global coordinating body for legal issues, technical co-operation, and maritime security including anti-piracy efforts. For more information, see: http://www.imo.org/.

[75] IMO Resolution A. 1002(25) "calls Upon Governments in the region to conclude, in co-operation with the Organization, and implement, as soon as possible, a regional agreement to prevent, deter and suppress piracy and armed robbery against ships."

[76] Resolution 1851 "encourages all states and regional organizations fighting piracy and armed robbery at sea off the coast of Somalia to consider creating a center in the region to coordinate information relevant to piracy and armed robbery at sea off the coast of Somalia."

[77] Meeting minutes available at: http://www.fco.gov.uk/resources

[78] Djibouti, Ethiopia, Kenya, Madagascar, Maldives, Seychelles, Somalia, the United Republic of Tanzania, and Yemen signed the code of conduct in January.

[79] Text available at: http://www.recaap.org/about/pdf/ReCAAP%20Agreement.pdf. Sixteen signatories include the People's Republic of Bangladesh, Brunei Darussalam, the Kingdom of Cambodia, the People's Republic of China, the Republic of India, the Republic of Indonesia, Japan, the Republic of Korea, the Lao People's Democratic Republic, Malaysia, the Union of Myanmar, the Republic of the Philippines, the Republic of Singapore, the Democratic Socialist Republic of Sri Lanka, the Kingdom of Thailand, and the Socialist Republic of Vietnam.

[80] A diagram of ReCAAP-ISC reporting and response procedures is available at: http://www.recaap.org/about/pdf/Information_Flow_Response_chart.pdf.

[81] Resolution 1851 "invites" states and regional organizations "to conclude special agreements or arrangements with countries willing to take custody of pirates in order to embark law enforcement officials ("shipriders") from the latter countries, in particular countries in the region, to facilitate the investigation and prosecution of persons detained as a result of operations conducted under [the] resolution."

[82] Transcript, UNODC Executive Director Antonio Maria Costa testimony before the House Foreign Affairs Subcommittee on International Organizations, Human Rights, and Oversight, May 14, 2009.

[83] One knot is unit of measurement equivalent to one nautical mile per hour or 1.15 miles per hour.

[84] The term 'freeboard' refers to the distance between the waterline and the main deck of the ship.

[85] Best Management Practices to Deter Piracy in the Gulf of Aden and off the Coast of Somalia, Version 2, August 2009. Available at: http://www.icc-ccs.org/images 21-8-2009.pdf.

[86] Available at: http://www.icc-ccs.org/index.php?option=com_content&view=article&id

[87] AFRICOM's AOR includes all African countries except Egypt, which remained in the AOR of CENTCOM after that command transferred responsibilities for the Horn of Africa countries to AFRICOM in 2008. For more information see CRS Report RL 34003, *U.S. Africa Command: U.S. Strategic Interests and the Role of the U.S. Military in Africa*, by Lauren Ploch.

[88] U.S. AFRICOM/Republic of Seychelles, Office of the President, "Seychelles President James Michel Hails Strengthening of Surveillance Cooperation with the United States," August 20, 2009.

[89] According to the Administration justification for the supplemental request, "funding may also be directed towards Security Sector Reform (SSR) efforts. Some funding will pay for equipment and logistical support for training efforts for Somali troops by Tanzania, Uganda, Rwanda, and other nations in the region that will implement the training activities." The Administration also is seeking authority to transfer up to $50 million in supplemental Contributions for International Peacekeeping Activities (CIPA) funding to the PKO account for Somalia, if necessary.

[90] Testimony of then-Acting Undersecretary of State for International Security and Arms Control Stephen Mull before the House Armed Services Committee, March 5, 2009.

[91] Convention on the High Seas, 13 U.S.T. 2312; T.I.A.S. 5200; 450 U.N.T.S. 82. Signed at Geneva, April 29, 1958. Entered into force September 30, 1962.

[92] United Nations Convention on the Law of the Seas (UNCLOS), 21 I.L.M. 1261. Convention adopted December 10, 1982. Entered into force November 16, 1994 (the United States is not a party to the Agreement).

[93] Convention for the Suppression of Unlawful Acts Against the Safety of Maritime Navigation, T.I.A.S. Signed at Rome, March 10, 1988. Entered into force March 1, 1992 (for the United States March 6, 1995).

[94] The United Nations Convention on the Law of the Sea (A historical perspective), available at http://www.un.org/Depts/los/convention_agreements/convention_historical_perspective.htm.

[95] Convention on the High Seas at Article 14; UNCLOS at Article 100.

[96] UNCLOS at Article 101. (The definition is, with a minor grammatical change, the same definition found in the Convention on the High Seas (Article 14).

[97] Convention on the High Seas at Article 22.

[98] Convention on the High Seas at Article 19; UNCLOS at Article 105.

[99] *Id.*

[100] International Maritime Organization statement on aims for the Convention for the Suppression of Unlawful Acts Against the Safety of Maritime Navigation. Available at http://www.imo.org/.

[101] *Id.*

[102] Convention for the Suppression of Unlawful Acts Against the Safety of Maritime Navigation at Article 5.

[103] 18 U.S.C. § 1651 *et seq.*

[104] 18 U.S.C. §§ 1651 and 1652.

[105] For one review and discussion of these legal questions from a U.S. military point of view, see Cmdr. James Kraska and Capt. Brian Wilson, "Fighting Piracy," *Armed Forces Journal*, February 1, 2009 (expressing view that international and regional cooperation, not armed force, is the long-term solution to piracy).

[106] *See* http://www.smh.com.au/world/fate-of-teen-pirate-uncertain-20090414-a5ih.html.

[107] For example, under common law, children under the age of seven are conclusively presumed to be without criminal capacity, those who have reached the age of fourteen are treated as fully responsible, while as to those between the ages of seven and fourteen there is a rebuttable presumption of criminal incapacity. In addition jurisdictions have adopted juvenile court legislation providing that some or all criminal conduct by those persons under a certain age (usually eighteen) must or may be adjudicated in the juvenile court rather than in a criminal proceeding. LaFave & Scott, Criminal Law §4.11 (2d ed. 1986).

[108] The U.S. State Department provided CRS with documents on the status of piracy trials in Kenya in September 2009.

[109] U.S. Department of Transportation Maritime Administration Advisories are available at: http://www.marad.dot.gov/news_room_landing_page/maritime

[110] U.S. Department of Transportation Maritime Administration Advisory #: 2009-07, Gulf of Aden, Red Sea and Indian Ocean Transit, September 9, 2009.

[111] International Maritime Organization, "Guidance to shipowners and ship operators, shipmasters and crews on preventing and suppressing acts of piracy and armed robbery against ships," MSC1/Circ.1334, June 23, 2009.

[112] International Maritime Bureau-Piracy Reporting Center, Best Management Practices, August 2009. Available at: http://www.icc-ccs.org/images 21-8-2009.pdf.

[113] Most of the concerns listed here are discussed in John W. Miller and Paulo Prada, "Attack Raises Debate On Guns For Sailors," *Wall Street Journal*, April 11, 2009; and Keith Bradsher, "Rescue Fuels Debate Over Arming Crews," *New York Times*, April 13, 2009.

[114] Katharine Houreld, "Private Ship Escorts Guard Against Pirates," *Navy Times.com*, June 5, 2009. For additional discussions of issues relating to arming of merchant ships, see Keith Bradsher, "Rescue Fuels Debate Over Arming Crews," *New York Times*, April 13, 2009; and John W. Miller and Paulo Prada, "Attack Raises Debate On Guns For Sailors," *Wall Street Journal*, April 11, 2009.

[115] Revised guidance on combating piracy agreed by IMO Maritime Safety Committee, Maritime Safety Committee - 86th session: 27 May - 5 June 2009.

[116] P.L. 90-629, 90 Stat. 744 (22 U.S.C. § 2778) (Arms export control is addressed in Chapter 39 of Title 22 of the *United States Code* (22 U.S.C. §§ 275 1-2799aa-2)).

[117] 22 C.F.R. §§ 120-130.

[118] A 'U.S. person' is defined at 22 C.F.R. §120. 14 and §120.15, as a "natural person who is a lawful permanent resident as defined by 8 U.S.C. § 1 101(a)(20) or who is a protected person as defined by 8 U.S.C. § 1324b(a)(3). It also means any corporation, business association, partnership, society, trust, or any other entity, organization or group that is incorporated to do business in the United States. It also includes any governmental (federal, state, local) entity."

[119] 22 C.F.R. pt. 121.

[120] The term 'United States' is defined at 22 C.F.R. § 120.13, as "when used in the geographical sense, includes the several states, the Commonwealth of Puerto Rico, the insular possession of the United States, the District of Columbia, the Commonwealth of the North Mariana Islands, any territory or possession over which the United States exercises any powers of administration, legislation, and jurisdiction."

[121] 22 C.F.R. § 120.17(a).

[122] 22 C.F.R. § 121.1.

[123] 22 C.F.R. § 123.18(c).

[124] *Id.*

[125] 22 C.F.R. § 126.1.

[126] John B. Perkins III, "Protect Our Mariners," *Washington Times*, August 30, 2009: B1.

[127] Christopher Torchia, "Western Nations Weigh Arming Civilian Ships," *NavyTimes.com*, August 13, 2009.

[128] Testimony of Arthur J. Volkle, Jr., Vice President, American Cargo Transport, Inc., before the House Committee on Transportation and Infrastructure Subcommittee on Coast Guard and Maritime Transportation, May 20, 2009.

[129] According to the A.M. Best Company, the U.S. property/casualty insurance industry's reported surplus, a measure of claims-paying capacity or capital, declined by about $62.3 billion or 12%, at year-end in 2008 to $455.6 billion from $517.9 billion at year-end 2007. While not all of the $455.6 billion is allocated to ocean marine insurance, the level of industry-wide surplus suggests U.S. private insurers have the overall financial resources to cover potential losses from incidences of ocean piracy.

[130] United States Navy, Commander, Combined Maritime Forces Public Affairs, "Combined Maritime Forces Issues New Alert to Mariners," April 7, 2009.

[131] Dr. Jun Bando, Maritime Security Coordinator/U.S. Africa Command Liaison, U.S. Department of State Bureau of African Affairs, "International Response to Piracy Expanded, Unified," *DipNote*, January 30, 2009.

[132] U.S. State Department Bureau of Political-Military Affairs, "Fact Sheet: United States Actions To Counter Piracy Off the Horn of Africa," September 1, 2009.

In: Ocean Piracy
Editor: Jacob E. Nelson
ISBN: 978-1-60741-495-7

Chapter 7

SOMALI PIRATE TACTICS

United States Maritime Administration

WHO ARE SOMALIA'S PIRATES?

- Former fishermen whose fishing areas have been exploited by foreign commercial fishing. Because of the lucrative ransoms, others factions joined in the activity.

WHO DO THEY WORK FOR?

- The pirates mainly work for themselves. Pirate gangs probably have relationships with corrupt officials to gather information.

WHO BENEFITS FROM PIRACY?

- The money is distributed within the clan to families and friends. Pirates have used revenues to buy luxury homes, cars, and additional wives.

How Did They Get So Good at This?

- Practice, practice, practice. This type of piracy has been going on since 1995.

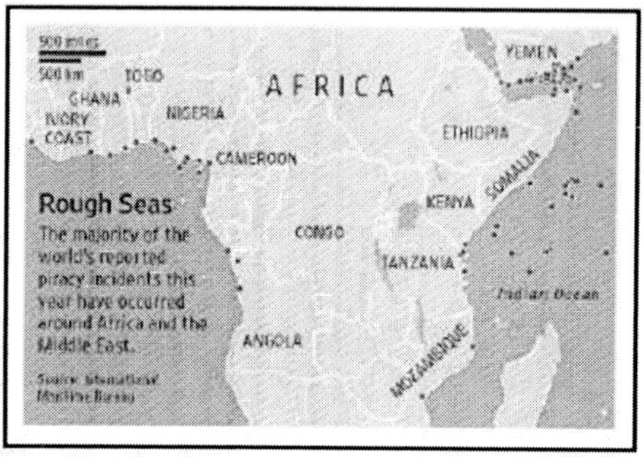

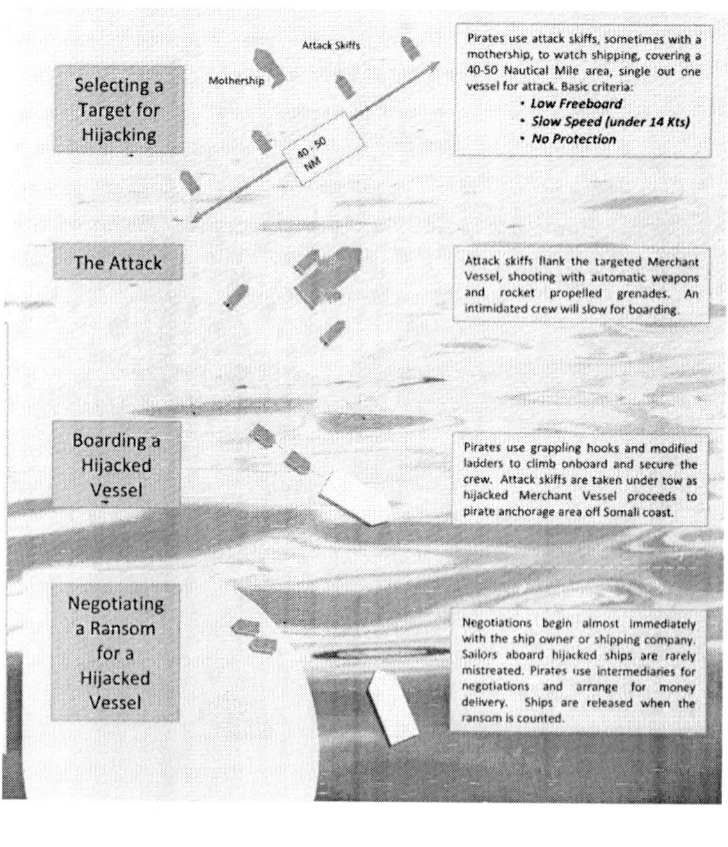

RECOMMENDED COUNTER - PIRACY MEASURES

- PREPARATION OF TRANSIT:
    - Notify MARLO 48hrs prior
    - ID a Crew muster area
    - Prepare list of Contacts
    - Add Security Detail
    - Pre-stage equipment
    - Practice piracy drills
- MAKING THE PASSAGE:
    - Use transit corridor (per 2008-05)
    - Check in with MARLO
    - Transit at highest speed possible
    - Transit at night
    - Mount fullest watch possible
- IF UNDER ATTACK:
    - Increase speed to maximum
    - Alter course
    - Man high-pressure hoses
    - Fire flares
    - Sound alarm signals
    - Notify area military forces
    - Notify MARLO
- WHEN IN DISTRESS:
    - Call for HELP on VHF-16 & MF/HF DSC
    - IMMEDIATELY contact UKMTO PHONE: +971 50 552 3215 EMAIL: ukmto@eim.ae
    - IF NO ANSWER CALL MARLO BAHRAIN PHONE +97339401395 EMAIL: *marlo.bahrain@me.navy.mil*
    - ACTIVATE SSAS (ship security alert system)

- Source: MARAD ADVISORY 2008-08/09

MARITIME ADMINISTRATION ADVISORIES

- 2008-04, Issued 4 December 2008 Alerts Mariners to be Vigilant in the Gulf of Aden (GOA)
- 2008-05, Issued 2 December 2008 Suggested Way Points for GOA Transit
- 2008-06, Issued 5 November 2008 Suggested Reporting Procedures
- 2008-07, Issued 5 November 2008 Suggested Anti-Piracy Precautions
- 2008-08, Issued 5 November 2008 Suggested Piracy Countermeasures
- 2008-09, Issued 7 November 2008 Suggested Anti-Piracy Distress Calling Procedures

IMB INCIDENT REPORTING

Contact the 24-hour Piracy Reporting Centre:

Tel: + 60 3 2078 5763
Fax: + 60 3 2078 5769
Telex: MA34199 IMBPCI
E-mail: imbkl@icc-ccs.org
24 Hours Anti Piracy HELPLINE Tel: +
60320310014

In: Ocean Piracy
Editor: Jacob E. Nelson
ISBN: 978-1-60741-495-7

Chapter 8

Somalia: Current Conditions and Prospects for a Lasting Peace

Ted Dagne

Summary

In October 2002, the Inter-Governmental Authority for Development (IGAD) launched a peace process designed to end factional fighting in Somalia, led by the government of Kenya. In September 2003, the parties agreed on a Transitional National Charter (TNC). In August 2004, a 275-member Transitional Parliament was inaugurated in Kenya. In October 2004, parliament elected Abdullahi Yusuf Ahmed as the new president of Somalia. In June 2006, the forces of the Islamic Courts Union (ICU) took control of the capital, Mogadishu. During the six-month rule by the ICU, Mogadishu became relatively peaceful, but efforts to bring peace did not lead to a major breakthrough. On December 28, 2006 Ethiopian troops captured Mogadishu with little resistance from the ICU.

The Ethiopian intervention led to more chaos and instability in Somalia over the past two years. Humanitarian, political, and security conditions continue to deteriorate across south-central Somalia. In the past two years, more than 15,000 civilians have been killed, an estimated 1.1 million people displaced, and 476,000 Somalis have fled to neighboring countries. In 2008, fighting between insurgent groups and Ethiopian-TFG forces intensified, and by late 2008, the TFG had lost control of most of south-central Somalia to insurgent groups. In November 2008, the Ethiopian government announced that its forces would pull out of Somalia by the end of 2008. In January 2009, Ethiopian forces completed their withdrawal from Somalia. In late December 2008, President Yusuf resigned from office and left for Yemen.

In June 2008, the TFG and the Alliance for the Re-Liberation of Somalia (ARS), a group dominated by members of the ICU, signed an agreement in Djibouti mediated by United Nations Special Envoy Ahmedou Ould-Abdullah. The parties agreed to a cease-fire, the withdrawal of Ethiopian forces, and the deployment of a United Nations peacekeeping force. Several towns are now administered by the ARS, including Jowhar and Beledweyne. A number of other towns, including the third largest town, Kismaayo, are now under the control of the Al-Shabaab, a group opposed to the TFG and the ARS-Dj ibouti faction. The next phase of the Somali conflict is likely to occur between the ARS and the Al-Shabaab. In February 2008, Secretary of State Condoleezza Rice designated Al-Shabaab as a Foreign Terrorist Organization. In January 2009, the Somali Parliament elected the leader of the ARS, Sheikh Sharif Sheikh Ahmad as president. In February 2009, President Ahmad appointed Omar Abdirashid Ali Sharmarke as prime minister.

Meanwhile, Somali pirates have intensified their attacks in the Gulf of Aden, carrying out attacks on over 90 commercial ships, and successfully hijacked over 35 ships in 2008. Currently an estimated 14-18 ships are under the control of the pirates, including a Saudi-owned supertanker, *Sirius Star*, and a Ukrainian-owned ship, *MV Faina*, with 33 T-72 tanks and other weapons. In January-February 2009, Somali pirates released a number of the hijacked ships, including the *MV Faina.* The pirates have earned more than $120 million in ransom payments, and have released a number of the ships and crew members. The United States, Russia, India, and several other countries have deployed warships to tackle piracy in the Horn of Africa region. Some insurgent leaders have warned the pirates to end their illegal activities and to release crew members and ships that they currently control. This report will be updated as circumstances warrant.

Recent Developments

Political Developments

In late December 2008, President Yusuf resigned from office and left for Yemen. President Yusuf was opposed to the Djibouti peace process and repeatedly clashed with his prime minister. In January 2009, the Somali Transitional Parliament elected the leader of the ARS, Sheikh Sharif Sheikh Ahmad as president. President Ahmad is seen by many Somalis as a leader with the best chance of bringing peace and stability to Somalia and as someone who can bring those elements outside the peace process to join the new government. In January 2009, President Ahmad went to Ethiopia and took part in the African Union (AU) summit where he was welcomed by member states. In 2006, Ethiopian forces attacked and forced out Ahmad's Islamic Court's Union from power. However, President Ahmad was warmly welcomed by Ethiopian authorities during the AU summit in Ethiopia.

In February 2009, President Ahmad appointed Omar Abdirashid Ali Sharmarke as prime minister. Sharmarke is the son of former President of Somalia, who was killed during the 1969 military coup. Sharmarke received overwhelming support in the Transitional Parliament. The appointment of Sharmarke provided important representation in the new government for the Darod clan. Sharmarke belongs to the same sub-clan, the Majertain, as former president Yusuf. Moreover, the Transitional Parliament was expanded and now includes an additional 149 members from the main opposition group, the ARS. Parliament also extended the mandate of the Transitional Federal Government by another two years. Some observers expressed concern about the size of the new parliament, while others argued that it was a necessary measure to make the parliament more inclusive.

Humanitarian and security conditions continue to deteriorate in south-central Somalia, despite some political progress and a recent peace agreement between the Somali Transitional Federal Government (TFG) and the Alliance for the Re-Liberation of Somalia (ARS), a group formed by former members of the Islamic Courts Union (ICU) and Somalis from different backgrounds. The ouster from power of the ICU by Ethiopian forces in December 2006 created a security vacuum that was soon occupied by the more radical elements of the ICU's military factions. The moderate leadership of the ICU became marginalized, splintered, and weakened over the past year. U.S., TFG, and Ethiopian officials labeled the entire leadership of the ICU as extremist and terrorist in 2006. Eighteen months later, however, the same officials supported the inclusion of some former ICU members in a U.N.-led peace process.

In May-June, 2008, TFG and ARS officials met in Djibouti under the auspices of the United Nations. Officials from the United States, Europe, the African Union, the Arab League, the Organization of Islamic Conference, and regional governments took part as observers during the talks in Djibouti. The parties agreed on a wide range of issues, including cessation of hostilities and a commitment to find a durable peace agreement.[1] The parties agreed to support the deployment of a United Nations peacekeeping force and the phased withdrawal of Ethiopian forces from Somalia. The agreement, however, links the withdrawal of Ethiopian forces with the deployment of a U.N. peacekeeping force, although Ethiopian forces have already withdrawn from some areas. In addition, in November 2008, the Ethiopian government announced that its forces would pull out of Somalia by the end of 2008. In January 2009, Ethiopian forces completed their withdrawal from Somalia. The parties also agreed to provide unhindered humanitarian access to civilians in need and to establish a Joint Security Committee to ensure implementation of security arrangements and create an interim joint security force.[2] The parties established a High Level Committee, chaired by the United Nations, to deal with political, justice, and governance issues.

The Djibouti agreement is complicated and has repeatedly been undermined by in-fighting within the TFG, insecurity, growing influence of insurgent groups, and limited support by the international community. The TFG forces are weak, ineffective, and seriously debilitated by defections. Over the past year, an estimated 40% of the police force, trained by the United Nations, left the force due to lack of payment. Some donor governments have withheld funds pledged to the TFG due to lack of transparency and human rights abuses. Infighting within the TFG, especially between then-Prime Minister Nur Adde and then-President Yusuf, weakened the TFG. In November 2007, Prime Minister Nur Adde replaced Ali M. Ghedi, a man seen by many Somalis as ineffective and highly partisan.

Prime Minister Nur Adde, who is seen by many Somalis and Somali observers as a key actor to bridge the gap between the TFG and the opposition, often clashed with President Yusuf. In July 2008, the prime minister dismissed the mayor of Mogadishu and Governor of Benadir region, Mohamed Dheere, because of mismanagement of funds. In protest, ten pro-Yusuf ministers resigned, triggering a crisis within the TFG. In August 2008, the prime minister and the president met in Ethiopia, and later reached an agreement on a number of issues. In Mid-December 2008, President Yusuf fired Prime Minister Nur and named Mohamed Mohamud Guled as the new prime minister. The prime minister has rejected his dismissal arguing that President Yusuf lacked the legal authority to dismiss him and that only Parliament has the power to dismiss the prime minister. On December 15, 2008, a majority of the Somali Parliament voted in support of Prime Minister Nur Adde. The government of Kenya imposed a travel ban and asset freeze against President Yusuf.

The ongoing Djibouti peace process aims to establish a new, inclusive government in Mogadishu.[3] The primary objective is to form a new National

Unity Government made up of Somalis from different backgrounds, including former members of the ICU. The parties also reportedly plan to expand the current 275-member parliament. The Somali Parliament has been inactive due to insecurity, defections, and infighting. The Djibouti peace process, however, faces serious challenges. The balance of military power on the ground has shifted in favor of the AlShabaab, the Youth, a group determined to expand its influence and control beyond Mogadishu. The Al-Shabaab, if successful in capturing Mogadishu, is likely to seek control of Somaliland and Puntland by military means.

Some of the military commanders of the ICU are likely to join forces with the Al-Shabaab. A negotiated settlement between the ICU and the Al-Shabaab is possible, with the withdrawal of Ethiopian forces and intervention by clan elders. Some of the Al-Shabaab leaders are currently engaged in talks with some members of the ICU. But the leaders of the Al-Shabaab are not fully known, with the exception of some. Some of the key commanders and leaders of the Al-Shabaab come from Somaliland. Ahmed Abdi Godane, who is on the U.S. terrorism list, is a key commander, who trained and fought in Afghanistan and comes from Somaliland. Mukhtar Robow, who is on the U.S. terrorism list, is the spokesman of the Al-Shabaab. Another key leader is Ibrahim Haji Jama, who is on the U.S. terrorism list, reportedly trained and fought in Afghanistan. In February 2008, Secretary of State Condoleezza Rice designated Al-Shabaab as a Foreign Terrorist Organization and as a Specially Designated Global Terrorist.

Security Conditions

In 2008, insurgent groups have stepped up attacks against Ethiopian and TFG forces in south- central Somalia. In some cases, TFG forces simply withdrew from some areas. As of late November 2008, insurgent groups were in control of most of south-central Somalia, including the third largest town, Kismaayo. Ethiopian and TFG forces, as well as the African Union Mission to Somalia (AMISOM), do not have control or presence outside Baidoa and Mogadishu. Even in the case of Mogadishu, the insurgents control some parts of Mogadishu and some of their forces are active outside the capital. The forces of the ARS are reportedly in control of Beledweyne and Jowhar, with some support from Ethiopian and TFG forces.[4] The Al-Shabaab forces also have expanded their military operations to other parts of Somalia and routinely assassinate opponents and government officials.

Security conditions are likely to deteriorate further in the coming months, despite the peace agreement between the TFG and the ARS. In late October 2008, simultaneous and well-coordinated suicide attacks in Puntland and Somaliland reportedly killed an estimated 20 people and injured many more. The targets of the attacks were the Ethiopian Consulate, the office of the United Nations Development Program (UNDP), and a security office close to the Presidential Palace. The suicide mission was reportedly carried out by members of the Al-Shabaab, although no organization claimed credit for the attacks. One of the suicide bombers is an American-Somali from Minneapolis, who, according to press reports, left the U.S. to take part in the suicide attacks. Reportedly, over a dozen Somali youth from Minneapolis have left the U.S, and some community leaders believe they went to Somalia to join the insurgency. There is no clear evidence of how many and for what purpose these Somalis left Minneapolis.[5] Over the past decade, many Somalis have returned to Somalia to work as journalists, humanitarian workers, and teachers. A number of these Somalis have been killed in the past two years by insurgents and security forces.

Human Rights and Humanitarian Conditions

In 2008, humanitarian and human rights conditions became worse than previous years, according to United Nations officials and Somali humanitarian workers. An estimated 1.1 million people have been displaced and more than 475,000 have fled to neighboring countries in the past two years. Human rights groups and Somali observers estimate more than 10,000 people have been killed over the past eighteen months. Civilians, humanitarian workers, journalists, and human rights advocates have been the primary targets of the insurgents, TFG, and Ethiopian security forces. According to Amnesty International, "rape, killings and looting have become widespread. Entire neighborhoods have been destroyed."[6] A number of Somali journalists covering the crisis in Somalia have been assassinated by insurgents and security forces over the past eighteen months. Dozens of humanitarian and human rights advocates have been killed, injured, or imprisoned by TFG and Ethiopian security forces. Because of these targeted attacks, many human rights advocates and journalists have fled Somalia to neighboring countries for safety.[7] Somalis working for international NGOs and foreign media have also been attacked by insurgents and TFG/Ethiopian security forces.

SOMALI PIRACY IN THE HORN OF AFRICA

Overview

Somali pirates have intensified their attacks in the Gulf of Aden, carrying out attacks on over 90 commercial ships, and successfully hijacked an estimated 40 ships in 2008. As of mid-February 200, an estimated 11-15 ships were under the control of the pirates, including a Saudi-owned supertanker, *Sirius Star*, and a Ukrainian-owned ship, *MV Faina*, which is carrying 33 T-72 tanks and other weapons, according to press reports. In January-February 2009, Somali pirates released several ships, including a Japanese-owned ship, *MV Chemstar,* and *the MV Faina.* The pirates have reportedly earned more than $120 million in ransom payments, and have released a number of ships and crew members. The United States, Russia, India, and several other countries have deployed warships to tackle piracy in the Horn of Africa region. In February 2009, the U.S. Navy arrested 16 suspected Somali pirates. In December 2008, the Indian Navy reportedly arrested 23 Somali and Yemeni pirates. Moreover, the Russian Navy also arrested a number of suspected Somali pirates.

In January 2009, the United States and Britain signed legal agreements with the Government of Kenya to extradite suspected pirates to be prosecuted in Kenya. Some insurgent leaders have warned the pirates to end the piracy and to release crew members and ships currently controlled by the pirates. On December 16, 2008, the United Nations Security Council passed a resolution authorizing the use of "all necessary measures" by foreign military forces to stop piracy in Somalia. The resolution authorizes military operations inside Somalia and in its airspace for one year, with the consent of the TFG.

Who Are the Pirates?

The number of Somali pirates is unknown. While there are more pirates now than previous years, the pirates do not seem to have a unified organization with clear command structure. Many of these pirates are reportedly fishermen and former militia members of the Somali warlords. The pirates primarily come from Puntland region of Somalia and are members of different clans. Some press reports have suggested that the pirates are being controlled and directed by the Islamic insurgents in south-central Somalia. There is no evidence, however, to support this assertion, and during the six months the ICU was in power, the leaders took measures to end piracy and other criminal activities. In November 2008, one of the top leaders of the insurgents, Sheik Hassan Aweys, called on the pirates to end their criminal activities, and other insurgent leaders threatened to take military action against the pirates. The pirates, however, are not operating alone, according to a number of Somali and regional sources. Some Somali businessmen and officials in Puntland are reportedly behind the piracy. The pirates are reportedly receiving valuable information about the types of ships, cargo, and timing from Somalis in the Persian Gulf.[8] They also possess sophisticated technology, including Global Position Systems (GPS), Automatic Identification System (AIS), and satellite phones.

The Views from Somalia

Some Somalis view the piracy crisis as a foreign problem with little impact on their daily life. Some argue that the piracy problem will continue as long as the ship-owners are willing to pay the pirates ransom. In the face of difficult economic conditions and growing humanitarian crisis, many Somalis resent the fact that the piracy problem has received a great deal of international attention. Some Somali community leaders contend that some Somalis get involved in criminal activities in order to survive, while many others have made these kinds of criminal activities a lifetime profession. Since the collapse of the Siad Barre government in 1991, Somalis have been principal victims of criminals. Somalis had to pay "taxes" to warlords in order to pass from one neighborhood to another. Humanitarian assistance convoys are routinely targeted by criminal elements, forcing humanitarian agencies to hire gunmen for protection. Many Somalis contend that in the absence of a better alternative, they have come to accept life with all the difficulties they face daily.[9]

Some Somalis argue that the fishermen have become pirates because their way of life was destroyed by illegal fishing and toxic waste dumping that has been ignored by foreign governments. In 2005, the United Nations Environment Program (UNEP) released a report documenting the damages done as a result of toxic waste dumping on Somalia's shores. According to a UNEP spokesman, "there's uranium radioactive waste, there's lead, there's heavy metals like cadmium and mercury, there's industrial waste, and there's hospital wastes, chemical wastes, you name it." According to the report, the primary reason for toxic dumping in Somalia is cost. The report states that it costs $2.5 per ton to dump toxic waste in Africa compared to $250 per ton to dump waste in Europe.[10] In July 2008, United Nations Special Envoy Ould-Abdallah stated that "because there is no (effective) government, there is so much irregular fishing from European and Asian countries." The Special Envoy argued that it is important to tackle these illegal activities by some countries, and not to solely focus on the problem of piracy.[11]

SOMALIA: FACTS & STATISTICS

Population: 9.5 million (2008 est.)
Growth rate: 2.85% (2008 est.)
Life expectancy: 49.2 years
Approximate size: slightly smaller than Texas
Capital: Mogadishu
Infant Mortality Rate: 110.97 deaths/1,000 live births (2008 est.)
HIV/AIDS, adult prevalence rate: 1% (2001 est.)
GDP, per capita: $600 (2007 est.)
GDP, real growth rate: 2.6% (2007 est.)
Ethnic groups: Somali, 85%; Bantu & other non-Somali, 15% (including Arabs, 30,000)
Religion: Sunni Muslim
Official language: Somali

Policy Options in Dealing with Piracy

The international community has responded to the threat of piracy by deploying warships to the Gulf of Aden. The United Nations Security Council has passed resolutions on piracy in the Horn of Africa. Since the deployment of these warships to the region, however, the number of hijacked ships has increased. Moreover, there has been no rescue operation as of November to free crew members and ships still under the control of the pirates. Somali community leaders and regional analysts argue that the groups most capable and best positioned to handle the piracy problem are the Islamic insurgents and the clan elders. The Islamic Courts dealt with this problem effectively when they were in power, according to senior leaders of the Islamic Courts and independent observers. The Islamic insurgents claim that they are opposed to these kinds of criminal activities for religious reasons. The Islamic leadership sees the piracy problem as a source of concern because they fear that they could erroneously or deliberately linked to the piracy phenomenon and become targets of punitive action by the international community. Another option is to provide quick and robust economic incentives to lure the unemployed away from piracy and other criminal activities.

Policy Options in Dealing with Political and Security Problems

The international community may consider engagement with the Islamic insurgents and clan elders to deal with the political and security problems facing Somalia. According to some observers, it is pivotal to strengthen the moderate elements of the Islamic movements discretely. Most observers believe that the Al-Shabaab can only be contained by another Islamic movement supported by clan elders. Some of the most influential leaders in the Al-Shabaab are on the U.N. and U.S. Terrorism List. Some observers argue that removing some of these individuals from the Terrorism List in exchange for some concessions, including an end to the insurgency and acceptance of a negotiated settlement, should be considered as an option. One of the key players in facilitating the Djibouti talks was a Somali man on a United Nations Terrorism List. According to U.N. officials, that man is no longer on the Terrorism List.

Some of the leaders in the Al-Shabaab are determined to continue their military campaign and not inclined to participate in negotiations. According to some experts, targeted measures, including sanctions and assassination of the most extreme elements of the Al-Shabaab, could pave the way for other moderate leaders to emerge. However, others believe that this option is likely to backfire in the short term and increase anti-western violence. Another option is to refer some of these individuals to the International Criminal Court (ICC) for war crimes. The most effective way of containing the extremists, most observers contend, is to look for a Somali-led solution, both political and military. The TFG, Islamic Courts, Somaliland, Puntland, and other moderate Somali forces could form a coalition to contain the advances of the most extreme elements of the AlShabaab politically and militarily. Such a coalition is likely to get the support of the Somali population rather than a peacekeeping force. The coalition can be assisted by neighboring countries. A Somali-led initiative would take away one of the most powerful justifications used by the Al-Shabaab to wage war, the presence of foreign forces. A unified regional approach is pivotal, however. Most believe that Eritrea has leverage over some of the influential Islamic leaders, some of whom are in Eritrea. The ARS was founded in Eritrea, and some of its leaders are now engaged in the U.N.-led negotiation in Djibouti.

The Alliance for the Re-Liberation of Somalia

In September 2007, Somalis from the Diaspora, civil society, opposition groups, and former members of parliament met in Eritrea and formed the Alliance for the Re-Liberation of Somalia (ARC). More than 400 people participated at the founding conference. The Al-Shabaab, the Youth, did not participate, and later condemned the leadership of the Alliance. The Alliance significantly reduced the dominance of the Council of the Islamic Courts and brought into the leadership people from civil society, women's groups, and former members of the TFG. The Alliance also brought into the coalition people from different regions and clans of Somalia. In addition, individuals, such as Hassan Aweys, considered by the west as extremists or terrorists, were not given leadership positions. According to the Alliance, the main objectives of the coalition are:

- The liberation of Somalia from Ethiopia.
- Somali solutions by Somali-stake-holders through dialogue and peaceful means.
- To establish a National Government "completely devote its utmost care to the welfare of the people, protect its rights, properties and promote its spiritual and material development."[12]
- Fighting crimes and violence targeted against civilian population, such as killing, raping, pillaging, dislodging and displacing.
- Resettlement of displaced people.
- Organize general elections once peace and security is established.

In March 2008, the Chairman of the Alliance in a letter to the President of the Security Council wrote "A peacekeeping mission would be possible only after the departure of the Ethiopian troops. Experience has shown that when peacekeepers are unilaterally imposed by the Security Council, they turn into peace enforcers. To avoid such a situation, the consent of the parties to the conflict is essential." In January 2008, the Alliance leadership informed a congressional delegation that the Alliance will accept a humanitarian cease-fire, zones of tranquility, and negotiations with the TFG and others once Ethiopian forces are replaced by a neutral force. This position led to a split of the Alliance. Many of the top leaders of the Alliance left Eritrea for Djibouti to participate in the U.N.-sponsored negotiations.

Table 1. The Leadership of the Executive Council of the ARS before the Split

Name	Title	Affiliation
Sheikh Sharif Sheikh Ahmed	Chairman	Somali Council of the Islamic Courts (SCIC)
General Jama Mohmed Galib	Vice Chairman	Civil Society
Zakaria Hagi Mohamud Abdi	Vice Chairman	Parliament
Prof. Ibrahim Hassan Addou, Ph.D.	Foreign Affairs Advisor	SCIC
Dr. Mohamed Ali Dahir	Administration Consultant	Somali intellectual
Prof. Abdirahman Ibrahim Ibbi	Assistant to the Chairman	Parliament
Ambassador Yusuf H. Ibrahim	Foreign Affairs Secretary	Parliament
Ahmed Abdullahi Sheikh	Information Secretary	Civil Society
Col. Omar Hashi Aden	Interior Secretary	Parliament
Ahmed Abdullahi Sheikh	Information Secretary	Civil Society
Col. Omar Hashi Aden	Interior Secretary	Parliament
Abdifitah Mohamed Ali	Finance Secretary	SCIC
Yusuf Mohamed Siad	Defense Secretary	SCIC
Dr. Mohamed Ahmed Mohamed, MD	Health Secretary	Civil Society
Dr. Mohamed Ali Ibrahim, Ph.D.	Justice Secretary	SCIC
Dr. Mohamud Abdi Ibrahim	Relief and Rehabilitation Secretary	
Mrs. Fowsia Mohmed Sheikh	Human Rights Secretary	Parliament
Mohamud Ahmed Tarzan	Planning & Training Secretary	Diaspora
Abdulkadir Mohmed Dhakane	Education Secretary	Parliament
Mohmed Ibrahim Garyare	Social Affairs Secretary	Diaspora
Ahmed Abdulle Hussain	Reconciliation Secretary	SCIC
Abdullahi Sheikh	Auditing Secretary	SCIC

BACKGROUND: 2006-2008

On December 24, 2006, Ethiopian and TFG forces launched a military campaign against the forces of the ICU, a group that took over power in Mogadishu, the capital of Somalia, in June 2006. On December 28, 2006 Ethiopian troops captured Mogadishu with little resistance from the ICU. The ICU leadership decided a day before the Mogadishu attack to leave the city in order to avoid bloodshed and the destruction of Mogadishu, according to a senior official of the ICU.[13] On January 1, 2007, the ICU lost its last stronghold, Kismaayo, after its forces withdrew to an area near the Kenyan border, although most of its fighters and leaders either simply melted into society throughout Somalia or fled to neighboring countries. Some of the top leaders of the ICU are in Yemen, Djibouti, Kenya, and Somalia.[14] In late January, the Chairman of the Executive Committee of the Somali Council of Islamic Courts (SCIC), formerly known as ICU, Sharif Sheik Ahmed, traveled to Kenya. On January 24, 2007, the U.S. Ambassador to Kenya, Michael Ranneberger, reportedly met with Sheik Ahmed. Other leaders of the Courts have also been approached by U.S. officials as part of a new strategy to reach out to Court officials and others to participate in proposed negotiations among Somali groups and the TFG.

The Ethiopian military intervention, while it has accomplished its military objective of ousting the Courts from Mogadishu and other areas the Courts controlled, has been criticized by governments and regional organizations. The African Union, the European Commission, the Arab League, and others have called for the deployment of a United Nations peacekeeping force. Ethiopian officials argued that their military action is justified because the Islamic Courts posed a serious threat to Ethiopia and regional stability, and because the Islamic Courts is an extremist, Jihadist group. Ethiopian and U.S. officials also have accused the Courts of being influenced or tied to well known terrorist individuals and Al Qaeda. Islamic Courts officials have repeatedly rejected these allegations and on a number of occasions have offered to work with U.S. officials, according to one senior Courts official. Allegations about the presence of the three suspects involved in the bombings of the U.S. embassies in Tanzania and Kenya in 1998 have been made on many occasions over the years. However, the Islamic Courts did not exist as an organized group when these allegations were made. Those in charge of Mogadishu and other areas in southern Somalia were the warlords who were and in some cases still are ministers in the current Transitional Federal Government.

On January 8, 2007, the United States Air Force, using AC-130 gun ships, attacked several locations in southern Somalia, reportedly to kill the three terror suspects in the 1998 U.S. embassy bombings in Kenya and Tanzania. Reportedly, the United States launched another attack the following day, although U.S. officials deny any further attacks by its forces. The British humanitarian group, Oxfam, stated in a press release that an estimated 70 people were killed in the bombings and vital water resources were destroyed in Afmadow district. A number of governments criticized the U.S. attacks, including officials in Europe and the Government of Djibouti, where U.S. forces are currently stationed. Djiboutian Foreign Minister Mahmoud Ali Yusuf told the BBC that the raid was counterproductive to achieving peace. He also stated that his government had not been informed about the air strikes. According to a *New York Times* article, the United States actively coordinated with Ethiopian forces in targeting suspected terrorists and Islamic Union forces.[15] U.S. Special Operations troops from Task Force 88 were reportedly deployed to Ethiopia and entered Somalia. Moreover, the United States reportedly shared intelligence with Ethiopian military and used an airstrip in Eastern Ethiopia to launch attacks inside Somalia. A senior Ethiopian government official denied that there was any coordination with U.S. forces.

Ethiopian troops have come under attack, and a number of Ethiopian soldiers have been killed by snipers or in ambushes. Some Somalis and human rights advocates are concerned over what some people refer to as a witch hunt by TFG and Ethiopian security forces. Ethiopian and TFG security forces reportedly have been going house to house arresting Oromos (an Ethiopian ethnic group), supporters of the Islamic Courts, and members of the TFG considered not supportive of the new Somali government and the Ethiopian intervention. The government of Kenya has deported dozens of Somalis and other nationals to TFG officials and Ethiopian security forces, according to Kenyan sources. In one particular case, Kenyan officials reportedly blindfolded and handcuffed 30 individuals and returned them to Mogadishu, where these detainees were taken by Ethiopian and TFG security personnel to unknown locations, according to Somali sources and government officials in the region. A number of Kenyan Muslims that were in Ethiopian detention were released in 2008.

On January 17, 2007, the Transitional Federal Parliament ousted the Speaker of Parliament, Sharif Hassan Sheik Adan, from his position. The former Speaker, who has been a vocal critic of the Ethiopian intervention and the U.S. air strike, has a strong following in Mogadishu and has been active in reaching out and engaging the Islamic Courts officials when they had control over Mogadishu. U.S. Assistant Secretary of State for Africa Jendayi Fraser stated in mid-January 2007 that "the no-confidence motion brought against the Parliament Speaker is likely to have a negative impact on this process of dialogue."[16] In late January, the TFG elected Sheikh Adan Mohamed Nur Madobe, a former warlord and an ally of President Abdullahi Yusuf, as Speaker of Parliament.

Peacekeeping Mission: Background

On December 6, 2006, the United Nations Security Council passed Resolution 1725, "reiterating its commitment to a comprehensive and lasting settlement of the situation in Somalia through the Transitional Federal Charter, and stressing the importance of broad-based and representative institutions and of an inclusive political process, as envisaged in the Transitional Federal Charter." U. N. Security Council Resolution 1725 further called for "all Member States, in particular those in the region, to refrain from any action in contravention of the arms embargo and related measures, and should take all actions necessary to prevent such contravention." Moreover, the Security Council expressed its "willingness to engage with all parties in Somalia who are committed to achieving a political settlement through peaceful and inclusive dialogue, including the Union of Islamic Courts." The Security Council, acting under Chapter VII of the Charter of the United Nations, authorized the Inter-Governmental Authority for Development (IGAD) and the African Union to establish "a protection and training mission in Somalia." U. N. Security Council Resolution 1725 specifically stated that countries bordering Somalia "would not deploy troops to Somalia."

At the African Union Summit in late January 2007, several African countries pledged to contribute troops for a peacekeeping mission in Somalia. Ghana, Nigeria, Burundi, Uganda, and Malawi have pledged troops. The African Union is facing difficulties getting governments to make serious troop contributions for the mission. Observers contend that without a negotiated settlement with groups still outside the TFG, it will be difficult to maintain peace and stability in Somalia. As of November 2008, there were an estimated 3,400 AU peacekeeping troops in Somalia from Uganda and Burundi. The African Union peacekeeping mission is mandated to:

- support dialogue and reconciliation in Somalia, working with all stakeholders,
- provide, as appropriate, protection to the TFIs and their key infrastructure, to enable them carry out their functions,
- assist in the implementation of the National Security and Stabilization Plan of Somalia, particularly the effective reestablishment and training of

all inclusive Somali security forces, bearing in mind the programs already being implemented by some of Somalia's bilateral and multilateral partners,

- provide, within capabilities and as appropriate, technical and other support to the disarmament and stabilization efforts,
- monitor, in areas of deployment of its forces, the security situation,
- facilitate, as may be required and within capabilities, humanitarian operations, including the repatriation and reintegration of refugees and the resettlement of IDP s, and
- protect its personnel, installations and equipment, including the right of self-defense.[17]

On February 20, 2007, the U.N. Security Council passed resolution 1744 reiterating its support for the Transitional Federal Institutions and authorizing the African Union to establish a mission in Somalia. Resolution 1744 calls for "a national reconciliation congress involving all stakeholders, including political leaders, clan leaders, religious leaders, and representatives of civil society." The resolution, while it welcomed the withdrawal of Ethiopian troops from Somalia, did not include a provision that restricts the participation of Somalia's immediate neighbors in the peacekeeping operation as resolution 1725 did.

The Security Council unanimously adopted Resolution 1772 on August 20, 2007, authorizing the African Union to maintain its operation in Somalia for an additional six months. The resolution also authorized peacekeeping forces on the ground to take all necessary measures to support and protect those involved in the Reconciliation Congress. Finally, Resolution 1772 called on all Member States, especially those in close proximity to Somalia, to comply with the arms embargo that was established in 1992 by Resolution 733.

THE ISLAMIC COURTS UNION

In early 2006, factional violence in Mogadishu once again erupted, killing hundreds of civilians and displacing many more people. The surge in violence was between militia loyal to the Islamic Courts and a self-proclaimed anti-terrorism coalition backed by powerful local warlords. The fighting in Mogadishu erupted when the forces loyal to a well known warlord and then Minister of National Security of the TFG, Mohamed Qanyare, attacked one of the Courts. The fighting received unusual attention in Somalia and in the region due, in large part, to reports that the warlords were backed by the United States government. The Bush Administration acknowledged that Washington was assisting "responsible individuals" to help bring stability and fight terrorism in Somalia. Assistant Secretary of State for Africa, Jendayi Fraser reportedly stated that the United States "will work with those elements that will help us to root out Al Qaeda and prevent Somalia becoming a safe haven for terrorists."[18] In late June 2006, Fraser stated that the United States has three major policy goals in Somalia: counter-terrorism efforts, creation of an effective government, and responding to the humanitarian needs of the Somali people.

On February 18, 2006, the Alliance for the Restoration of Peace and Counter-Terrorism (ARPCT) was created. Very little is known about ARPCT, although the founders of the Alliance are known warlords who contributed to numerous armed clashes and instability in Somalia over the past decade. Members of the Alliance reportedly include Bashir Rage, Mohammed Qanyare Afrah, Muse Sudi Yalahow, Omar Finnish, and Abdirashid Shire Ilqyete. These actors were seen by many Somali groups as major obstacles to the creation of central authority in Mogadishu, as agreed to by all major Somali groups under the IGAD peace agreement in 2004. In early June 2006, Prime Minister Ali Mohamed Gedi dismissed four ministers from the Transitional Federal Government belonging to ARPCT.

These ministers include Mohamed Qanyare (National Security Minister), Musa Sudi Yalahow (Commerce Minister), Issa Botan Alin (Rehabilitation Minister), and Omar Finnish (Minister for Religious Affairs). The warlords were dismissed because they reportedly ignored calls by Prime Minister Ghedi's government to stop the fighting in Mogadishu. The Islamic Courts leaders argued then that the TFG did nothing to challenge these warlords and kept them in senior positions in the TFG until the Islamic Courts defeated the warlords in Mogadishu. In late July 2006, members of the TFG parliament complained that the U.S. government bypassed the TFG and provided support to the warlords, the same warlords who obstructed peace in Somalia. A member of the TFG parliament told a U.S. Congressional delegation in August 2006 that "you cannot fight terrorism by supporting warlords."[19]

In early June 2006, the forces of the Islamic Courts captured Mogadishu, forcing ARPCT militia to flee the capital. The chairman of the Islamic Courts, Sharif Shaykh Ahmed, stated that his group would negotiate with the TFG. In response to accusations that the Islamic Courts Union was associated with or had harbored international terrorist elements, Shaykh Ahmed stated that "we are not terrorists and we will not allow anyone to hijack the capital. We have said hundreds of times that America's talk of terrorism in Somalia is fabricated and serves suspicious political purposes."[20]

The forces of the Islamic Courts Union strengthened and expanded areas under their control after the defeat of the warlords in Mogadishu. The Islamic Courts forces captured the towns of Jowhar and Beledweyne in mid-June 2006. Moreover, for the first time in years, Mogadishu became relatively peaceful, and the Islamic Courts received support from the population in areas it controlled. The level of support enjoyed by the Islamic Courts is difficult to measure, although the group had constituencies from multiple sub-clans and had broad support among Somali women. According to Somali sources in Mogadishu and Islamic Courts officials, the people provided crucial support by feeding their forces and working with Islamic Courts officials in bringing peace and stability. During the Mogadishu fighting, women supporters of ICU played important roles. Since the Islamic Courts largely functioned as providers of social services, the Courts did not maintain a large fighting force. The warlords maintained a robust force in different parts of Mogadishu, with heavy weapons and "technicals" (machine-guns mounted on pickup trucks). The Islamic Courts group had only four technicals when the fighting erupted with Qanyare and other warlords, according to a senior Courts official. The ICU success in Mogadishu effectively led to the collapse of the ARPCT and forced the warlords to flee.

Negotiations between the Transitional Federal Government and the Islamic Courts in Sudan did not lead to a major breakthrough, although the talks ended speculation that the Islamic Courts rejected negotiations. The Islamic Courts leaders stated that they would work with the Baidoa-based transitional government, although disagreement on key issues remained. In June 2006, the transitional parliament voted in favor of a foreign peacekeeping force. But this move was rejected by some Islamic Courts leaders as being unnecessary and counter-productive. Earlier, in 2005, the African Union had approved a proposal for Uganda and Sudan to deploy a peacekeeping force to Somalia under the auspices of the IGAD. The deployment did not take place in large part because of the refusal of the United Nations Security Council to remove a United Nations arms embargo on Somalia. The Bush Administration did not support the lifting of the arms embargo, although the United Nations Security Council did provide the necessary exemption in December 2006.

In mid-June, an International Somalia Contact Group, consisting of the United States, Norway, United Kingdom, Sweden, Italy, Tanzania, and the European Union, was formed and met to discuss the unfolding Somalia crisis. The United Nations, the African Union, the Arab League, and IGAD were also invited as observers. The Contact Group did not invite Somalia's immediate neighbors, in part due to Somali opposition and international concern that these countries are engaged in activities in support of or against some groups in Somalia. In a press release after its first meeting, the Contact Group stated that "the goal of the International Contact Group will be to encourage positive political developments and engagement with actors inside Somali to support the implementation of the Transitional Federal Charter and Institutions. The Contact Group will seek to support efforts, within the framework of the Transitional Federal Institutions, to address the humanitarian needs of the Somali people, establish effective governance and stability, and address the international community's concern regarding terrorism." Meanwhile, in early January 2007, the International Contact Group on Somalia issued another communiqué strongly urging that it is "essential that an inclusive process of political dialogue and reconciliation embracing representative clan, religious, business, civil society, women's, and other political groups who reject violence and extremism be launched without delay."

The Islamic Courts, while well received by the people in the areas the Courts controlled, received bad press coverage, especially in the West. The Courts' activities were often characterized as extremist and jihadist. The ICU was accused of shutting down cinemas and prohibiting women from working. Some of these measures were taken by the Courts, although for different reasons and not because of the Courts' alleged jihadist and extremist ideology. For example, movies were banned in the morning in response to requests from parents because Somali children were going to movies in the morning instead of school.[21] The ban on television did not take place, except for restrictions on watching soccer games late at night, according to Islamic Courts officials and Somali residents in Mogadishu. This measure was reportedly taken because of disturbances and fighting late at night. There is no evidence to support the allegation that women were prohibited from working. Islamic Courts officials point out that in the short time they were in power, they did more than restore law and order. Properties taken by warlords were returned to the rightful owners. For example, the family of President Yusuf reportedly returned to Mogadishu after almost sixteen years when the Courts restored order in the capital, according to an Islamic Courts official. Most important, they argue, they gave hope to the people of Somalia that after over a decade of violence they can live in peace.

THE LEADERSHIP OF THE SOMALI COUNCIL OF THE ISLAMIC COURTS

General knowledge of the top leadership of the Somali Council of the Islamic Courts (SCIC) is sketchy. The leadership was often referred to as jihadist, extremist, and at times terrorist by some observers without much evidence to support the allegations. For example, the assessment of the Islamic Courts by U.S. officials was that less than 5 percent of the Islamic Courts leadership can be considered extremist, according to a senior State Department official. In late June 2006, the Courts established a consultative body to function as the legislative (Shura) arm of the Courts. Hassan Dahir Aweys was elected to head the Legislative Council. Aweys was one of the top leaders of the now-defunct Al-Ittihad Al-Islamiya (AIAI—for more see below) and was designated by the Bush Administration as a terrorist. Sharif Sheik Ahmed, the leader of the Courts, was appointed chairman of the Council's Executive Committee to lead the day-to-day affairs of the Courts. Some observers and government officials have erroneously described Aweys as the leader of the Courts. However, the moderate leader of the Courts, Sharif Sheik Ahmed, was never replaced by Aweys. Some observers argued that referring to Aweys as the leader of the Courts was deliberately designed by some groups and governments to give the Courts a bad image.

The leadership of the Islamic Courts remained largely under the control of religious scholars and academics (see below). The focus by some observers and officials on three individuals, Aweys, Hassan Al-Turki, and Aden Ayro, may have been to show the Islamic Courts as a group controlled and influenced by these individuals. Al-Turki, a man born in the ethnically Somali Ogaden region of Ethiopia, was listed by the Bush administration as a terrorist because of his membership in Al- Ittihad. According to Courts officials, Al-Turki did not even hold a leadership position within the organization. Both Aweys and Al-Turki were placed on the list because of their membership in Al-Ittihad. There is no public record to support that these individuals were engaged in terrorist activities against U.S. or western interests. Ayro's role within the Courts was highly exaggerated since he did not have a leadership position in the organization. Ayro was often referred to as the leader of the Shibaab, the Youth, although there is no evidence to support that he was the leader of that group. Ayro was suspected of killing four aid workers in the breakaway region of Somaliland as well as a Somali scholar in Mogadishu named Abdulqadir Yahya. In May 2008, Ayro was killed in a U.S. air strike. Since the killing of Ayro, the insurgency has intensified its attacks and is now in control of many parts of south-central Somalia.

THE TOP LEADERS OF THE COURTS

The Executive Council

Sheikh Sharif Ahmed. Received a Law Degree from a University in Libya; served as President of Somali Intellectuals Associations; President of the District Court in Jowhar; President of Somali Council of Islamic Courts (SCIC); never been active in politics; married with two children. Now, Chairman of the ARS.

Abdurahman Muhamoud Farah. Vice President of SCIC. Studied in Mogadishu; a longtime advocate of peace and clan unity; never active in politics.

Abdulqadir Ali Omar. Vice President of SCIC. Longtime advocate of clan unity; religious scholar, and advocated against abuses by the warlords.

Ibrahim Hassan Addou. Foreign Secretary and a member of the Shura (Legislative Council) of the SCIC; Ph.D., MA, BA from American University, Washington, D.C.; Worked at American University from 1981 to 1992; held several positions at Benadir University in Mogadishu, including Vice President for Academic Affairs and President; married with three children.

The Legislative Council or Shura

Hassan Dahir Aweys. Speaker of the Shura. Former army officer in the Somali Armed Forces; fought in the Ethiopia-Somalia wars in the 1970s; former senior member of Al-Ittihad; fought against Ethiopia and Abdullahi Yusuf in the mid-1990s.

Omar Imam Abubakar. Number two in the Shura and effectively the most influential and active member of the Shura; received his Ph.D. from a University in Saudi Arabia; lectured in Mauritania and Somalia for many years.

Abdulahi Ali Afrah. Senior leader in the Shura. Holds a BA in Agriculture, longtime civil servant in the Siad Barre government; received an MA from a University in the U.S. and lived in Canada for many years.

Muhamoud Ibrahim Suleh. Senior member of the Shura, son of a well known religious leader.

LEADERSHIP OF THE TRANSITIONAL FEDERAL GOVERNMENT

Abdullahi Yusuf Ahmed. President of the TFG. A former senior army officer in Somalia; imprisoned by Siad Barre; attempted a coup against Barre in 1978 and later fled Somalia; led one of the first armed groups against Siad Barre with Ethiopian support; imprisoned by Ethiopian military dictator Mengistu Hailemariam in 1985 and released in 1991 after the ouster of the Mengistu regime by the current government; leader of the autonomous northeastern region of Puntland until 2001.

Ali Mohamed Ghedi. Prime Minister of the TFG. Studied in Somalia and Italy; A veterinarian by training; a lecturer and researcher at the Somali National University; no affiliation with warlords or political groups. Ghedi was replaced by Mr. Nur Adde in late 2007.

Sharif Hassan Sheik Adan. Former Speaker of Transitional Federal Parliament. Ousted from his position in January 2007; vocal critic of Ethiopia's intervention; had serious disagreements with President Yusuf; initiated negotiations with Courts leadership; a businessman and an advocate of reconciliation efforts. He joined the ARS in 2007.

Adan Mohamed Nur Madobe. Speaker of Parliament of the TFG. A former warlord and served as the Deputy Chairman of the Rahanweyn Resistance Army (RRA) and as Justice Minister of the TFG.

Hassan Muhammad Nur Shatigadud. Minister of Finance of the TFG; a known warlord and Chairman of the RRA.

Barre Adan Shire Hiiraale. Minister of defense. Served as the Chairman of the Juba Valley Alliance; Studied at West Point and served as army Colonel in the Barre regime; former commander of the Somali National Front (SNF).

Hussein Farah Aideed. Minister of Public Works and Housing. Served as Minister of Interior from 2005 to February 7, 2007; son of former faction leader Mohamed Farah Aideed; studied and lived in the United States; succeeded his father after his death in 1996. He left Somalia in 2007.

ETHIOPIA-SOMALIA RELATIONS

For over four decades, relations between successive Ethiopian governments and Somalia have been poor. Somalia invaded Ethiopia twice in the 1960s under Emperor Haile Selassie and in 1976 during the Mengistu Haile Mariam military rule. In the first war, the Ethiopian military commander General Aman Andom defeated Somali forces, but his request to go inside Somalia was rejected by the Emperor, and he was ordered to remain behind the border. The 1976 invasion of Ethiopia by Somali forces and Western Somali Liberation Front (WSLF) initially succeeded, leading to the capture of many Ethiopian towns by Somali forces. Somali forces briefly captured the third largest city, Dire Dawa, in Eastern Ethiopia. However, Ethiopian forces, with the support of Cuban and South Yemeni forces, were able to defeat the Somali forces, although elements of the Somali rebel forces remained in control of remote areas in the largely Somali inhabited areas of Ethiopia.

Both Ethiopian and Somali governments intervened in the internal affairs of the two countries, and successive governments on both sides supported each others' armed opposition groups. The current president of the Transitional Federal Government, President Abdullahi Yusuf, was one of the first to receive Ethiopia's assistance after he fled Somalia in the late 1970s. He was one of the first senior officials to challenge the Siad Barre government. Ethiopia was also the principal backer of the Somali National Movement (SNM), the group that liberated the northwest region of Somalia, currently known as Somaliland. The change of government in Ethiopia did not end Ethiopia's intervention in Somali affairs. The current government of Ethiopia became a key backer of a number of Somali factions and leaders, including the current president of the TFG, Abdullahi Yusuf, Hussein Aideed, and other Somali factions.

The Barre government was also a major sponsor of Ethiopian armed rebel groups. The current ruling party of Ethiopia, the Ethiopian People's Revolutionary Democratic Front (EPRDF), received assistance from Somali authorities and a number of the EPRDF leaders reportedly carried Somali-issued passports. Other rebel groups, including the Ogaden National Liberation Front

(ONLF) and the Oromo Liberation Front (OLF), also received assistance from Somalia. The ouster of the Siad Barre government and the absence of a central government in Somalia ended support for Ethiopian armed groups, although some Somali factions continue to support the ONLF. For most of the 1990s, Ethiopia's primary concern was Al-Ittihad in Somalia and its activities in support of the ONLF.

Al-Ittihad and ONLF carried out a number of attacks against Ethiopian targets, and Ethiopian security forces have violently retaliated against these groups and their supporters. The fighting with Al-Ittihad was triggered in the early 1990s when Ethiopian security forces brutally cracked down on the Ogaden National Liberation Front, a member of the first transitional government of Ethiopia. The ONLF joined the transitional government of Ethiopia in part because the Ethiopian Transitional Charter provided nations and nationalities the right to self determination; however, the ONLF push for self determination created tension between the ruling EPRDF and the ONLF.

In the early 1990s, Ethiopian security forces assassinated a number of ONLF leaders, cracked down on the organization, and moved the Ethiopian Somali Region capital from Gode to Jijiga, a central government stronghold. Members of the ONLF fled to Somalia and were embraced by Al-Ittihad, a fairly new group at that time. Hence, some observers view Al-Ittihad as a group largely concerned with domestic issues. Ethiopia's principal interest at that time was to ensure that a united Somalia did not pose a threat to Ethiopia and that the Somali-inhabited-region of Ethiopia remained stable. Ethiopian forces attacked Somalia a number of times over the past decade and often maintained presence inside Somali territory. Ethiopia's relationship with the current president of the TFG was strengthened when Yusuf backed Ethiopia's efforts against Al-Ittihad in the 1990s. The Ethiopian government's animosity towards the ousted Shura leader of the Islamic Courts, Sheik Aweys, is linked to Aweys' role as one of the leaders of Al-Ittihad fighting against Ethiopia and that of Abdullahi Yusuf.

In 2004, the government of Ethiopia released a report, *the Federal Democratic Republic of Ethiopia's Foreign Policy, Security Policy and Strategy*. The 158-page report covers a wide range of issues, including Ethiopia's assessment of its relations with Somalia. The report states that Somalia attacked Ethiopia twice in pursuit of its Greater Somalia ambition. The report notes that "at this time the Greater Somalia agenda has failed." Moreover, the Greater Somalia agenda no longer poses a serious threat to Ethiopia. The report contends that the factionalization of Somalia has allowed anti-peace and extremists elements to become strong, posing a threat to Ethiopia. In order to reduce the threat from some parts of Somalia, the Ethiopian government must pursue a policy of engagement and support to Puntland and Somaliland, according to the report. The report also recommends a policy of targeting those armed elements that threaten Ethiopian security. This report was released two years before the Islamic Courts emerged, although the report gave the same labels of extremist, terrorist, and anti-peace to groups that were dominant at that time.

SOMALIA: BACKGROUND (1991-2006)

In 1991, General Mohamed Siad Barre, who came to power through a military coup in 1969, was ousted from power by several Somali armed groups. Following the collapse of central authority in Mogadishu, rival Somali groups engaged in armed struggle for personal political power and prevented food and medicine from reaching innocent civilians suffering from drought and famine. An estimated 500,000 people died from violence, starvation, and disease as Somalia was wracked by continued internal chaos. On November 9, 1992, then-President George H.W. Bush authorized Operation Restore Hope, using the U.S. military, to safeguard non-governmental organizations (NGOs) and their efforts to provide humanitarian assistance to the suffering Somali civilian population.

The U.S.-led United Task Force (UNITAF) successfully subdued the warlords and armed factions and enabled NGOs to safely provide humanitarian relief to Somalis. In May 1993, UNITAF handed over the operation to the United Nations. The U.N. effort was known as United Nations Operation in Somalia (UNOSOM) II. In May 1993, UNOSOM II coalition forces were attacked by one of the factions in Mogadishu. On October 3, 1993, after a seventeen-hour battle between U.S. troops and Somali factions in Mogadishu, in which 18 U.S. Rangers were killed, President Clinton ordered the withdrawal of U.S. troops from Somalia. In March 1994, the United States completely pulled out of Somalia and, one year later, the United Nations pulled out the remaining peacekeepers. Since the withdrawal of United Nations forces in March 1995, Somalia has been without a central government and has been splintered into several regions controlled by clan-based factions.

Peace Processes

There have been 14 Somali reconciliation or peace conferences to bring an end to the fighting in Somalia since the early 1 990s. Some were held under the auspices of or were supported by the United Nations, or governments in the Horn of Africa. These efforts have largely failed to bring about lasting peace in Somalia. Moreover, competing efforts by international actors contributed to the failure of peace efforts in Somalia. In 1996, the Government of Ethiopia convened a peace process in the resort town of Sodere, Ethiopia. Many political actors and armed factions participated, although a few boycotted the peace process. The Sodere process collapsed when the government of Egypt convened another meeting of the Somali groups in Cairo in 1997. Subsequently, the Cairo initiative failed when yet another peace conference was convened by Somali factions in Bosaso, Somalia in 1998. In February 2000, IGAD approved a peace plan proposed by the government of Djibouti. In May 2000, the Somali Reconciliation Conference opened in Arta, Djibouti in which 400 delegates took part for several months of deliberation. The Arta process was boycotted by several powerful warlords, as well as the governments of Somaliland and Puntland.

On August 13, 2000, participants agreed to the creation of a Transitional National Government (TNG) and a Transitional National Assembly (TNA). On August 26, 2000, participants nominated Abdulqassim Salad Hassan as president of the TNG. In October 2002, the Inter-Governmental Authority for Development launched another peace process, led by the government of Kenya. An estimated 350 delegates from different regions of Somalia participated in the opening session of the conference in the Kenyan town of Eldoret. The Government of Somaliland boycotted the conference. In the first phase of the conference, the parties signed a temporary cease-fire, and agreed to respect and honor the outcome of the conference. The parties further agreed to establish a federal system of government and committed themselves to fight terrorism. In September 2003, the parties agreed on a Transitional National Charter, paving the way for a National Unity government.

In August 2004, a new Transitional Somali Parliament was inaugurated in Kenya. The 275-member parliament consists of the major political factions and seems to represent all the major clans of Somalia. The Transitional Charter allocated 61 seats for the major four clans and 31 seats for the small clans. The Charter also allocated 12% of the seats to women. The Charter accepted Islam as the national religion and agreed that *Sharia* law would be the basis of national legislation. In fact, previous Somali constitutions had similar provisions. In October 2004, the Somali Transitional Parliament elected Abdullahi Yusuf Ahmed as the new president of Somalia. The swearing in ceremony was attended by 11 heads of government from African countries and representatives from regional organizations and the United Nations.

In November 2004, President Abdullahi Yusuf Ahmed appointed Professor Ali Mohamed Gedi as prime minister. The transitional government, however, was not able to function effectively or move to Mogadishu in large part due to opposition from the warlords in Mogadishu, even though some of these warlords signed the agreement and were ministers in the government. The inability of the transitional government to establish effective control allowed warlords and clan factions to dominate many parts of Somalia until late December 2006. Some observers contend that the defeat of the warlords by the Islamic Courts paved the way for the establishment of central authority in Mogadishu.

National Reconciliation Conference

Somalia's recent peace effort, the National Reconciliation Congress, convened in the Shagaani district of Mogadishu on July 15, 2007 after being postponed twice for logistical and security reasons. The first phase of the conference came to an end on August 30, 2007. Somali Ambassador to Kenya Mohammed Ali Nur spoke optimistically about the results of the first phase of the conference at a news conference in Nairobi, Kenya: "I am happy to announce the declaration of peace agreement between major clans who are participating in the congress has already been signed... The transitional government has done and will continue doing its best to lead the process of reviving Somalia from the ashes of the vicious civil war." Whereas the first phase of the conference focused on the resolution of clan conflicts and disarmament, the second phase focused on issues such as power sharing, governance, sharing of natural resources, sea piracy, welfare, and internally displaced persons. The TFG did not take steps to address these issues since the Congress ended its meeting in late 2007.

Somalia: Safe Haven for Terrorist Groups?

The United States, Somali neighbors, and some Somali groups have expressed concern over the years about the spread of Islamic fundamentalism in Somalia. In the mid-1990s, Islamic courts began to emerge in parts of the country, especially in the capital of Mogadishu. These courts functioned as local governments and often enforced decisions by using their own Islamic militia. Members of the Al-Ittihad militia (see background below) reportedly provided the bulk of the security forces for these courts in the areas AIAI had a presence. The absence of central authority in Somalia created an environment conducive to the proliferation of armed factions throughout the country. Ethiopian security forces invaded Somalia on a number of occasions to disrupt the activities of Al-Ittihad and its allies or in support of certain armed factions.

Somali factions, including the so-called Islamic groups, often go through realignments or simply disappear from the scene. Very little is known about the leadership or organizational structure of these groups, including Al-Ittihad. There have been three known Islamic groups in Somalia whose prominence has alternately waxed and waned: Al-Ittihad Al-Islamiya (mentioned below), Al-Islah (Reform), and Al-Tabligh (Conveyers of God's Work). In 1995, a group called Jihad al- Islam, led by Sheikh Abbas bin Omar, emerged in Mogadishu, and gave the two main warlords, General Mohamed Farah Aideed and Ali Mahdi, an ultimatum to end their factional fighting. The group claimed at that time that it maintained offices in several countries, including Yemen, Pakistan, Kenya, and Sudan. Not much was heard subsequently from Jihad al-Islam, although a group of Somalis later formed the *Sharia* (Islamic law) Implementation Club (SIC) in 1996.

SIC's principal objective was to establish *Sharia* courts throughout the country. Some members of the Mogadishu-based former Transitional National Government (TNG) reportedly were key players in the establishment of these courts. Very little is known about al-Islah, although it is perceived as a group dominated by Hawiye clan businessmen. According to the State Department's 2006 *Country Reports on Terrorism*, "while numerous Islamist groups engaged in a broad range of activities operate inside Somalia, few of these organizations have any known links to terrorist activities. Movements such as Harakat al-Islah (al-Islah), Ahlu Sunna wal Jamaa (ASWJ), and Majma Ulimadda Islaamka ee Soomaaliya (Majma') sought power by political rather than violent means and pursued political action via missionary or charity work. Missionary Islamists, such as followers of the Tablighi sect and the "New Salafis" generally renounce explicit political activism. Other Islamist organizations became providers of basic health, education, and commercial services, and were perceived by some as pursuing a strategy to take political power."

U.S. officials have long expressed concern about the presence of known terrorist individuals in East Africa. Some observers contend that Somalia is being used as a transit and hiding place by some of these individuals, including Haroon Fazul, the leader of the 1998 and 2002 bombings, Saleh Nabhan, and Talha al-Sudani. But no Somali group has been directly linked to any terrorist attacks against the U.S. or its allies.

Al-Ittihad

Al-Ittihad was perhaps the most active and at one point most successful of all the Islamic groups. Al-Ittihad is an Islamic group whose principal ideology was to establish an Islamic state and to bring law and order by utilizing the Islamic court system. Founded in the late 1980s and early 1990s, Al-Ittihad unsuccessfully sought to replace clan and warlord politics with an Islamic state. In the early 1990s, Al-Ittihad had modest successes; for example, it administered territories under its control in the south. But Al-Ittihad never emerged as a major military or political force in Somalia. The clan-based groups and factions led by warlords in Mogadishu are secular and have been at odds with Al-Ittihad, even though some of these groups maintained tactical alliances from time to time with Al-Ittihad. Al-Ittihad's failure to maintain control over territories and spread its ideology led to a shift in strategy in the mid-1990s. Al-Ittihad abandoned its ambition to spread its ideology through military means and began to concentrate on providing social services to communities through Islamic schools and health care centers.

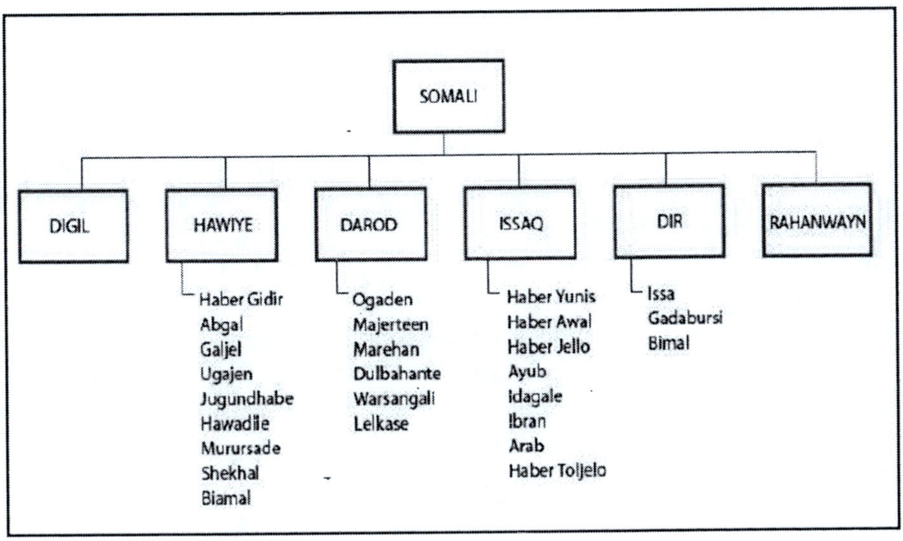

Figure 1. Major Somali Clans and Subclans

Al-Ittihad's social activities and religious objectives in Somalia seemed inconsistent with its activities in support of armed groups in the Somali-inhabited region of Ethiopia. In Ethiopia, Al- Ittihad was reportedly engaged in military activities in support of ethnic Somalis. Several anti- Ethiopian groups are active in the Somali region and Al-Ittihad cooperated with these groups in carrying out attacks against Ethiopian targets. In 1999, the Ogaden Islamic Union under the leadership of Muhammad Muallem Omar Abdi, the Somali People's Liberation Front under the leadership of Ahmed Ali Ismail, and the Western Somali Liberation Front under the leadership of Muhammad Haji Ibrahim Hussein formed a coalition called the United Front for the Liberation of Western Somalia, their term for the Somali-inhabited region of Ethiopia.[22] The Ogaden National Liberation Front was engaged in military activities in the region, and in the past formed alliances with other Ethiopian opposition groups.

Many Somali watchers believe that Al-Ittihad's strength was highly exaggerated and that information about its alleged links with international terrorist organizations is unreliable. The State Department's *Country Reports on Terrorism* stated in 2006 that "in recent years the existence of a coherent entity operating as AIAI (Al-Ittihad) has become difficult to prove." There is no reliable information or pattern of behavior to suggest that Al-Ittihad had an international agenda as was the case with the National Islamic Front (NIF) government of Sudan. Some observers note that if Al-Ittihad had a clear internationally-oriented agenda, its obvious ally in the region would be the NIF regime in Sudan or the Sudanese-backed Eritrean Islamic Jihad. The Sudanese regime did back regional extremist groups and international terrorist organizations, but there was no apparent relationship between the NIF and Al-Ittihad. Many Somalis often refer to Al-Ittihad's social services and the peace and stability that prevailed in the areas it controlled.

In late September 2001, the Bush Administration added Al-Ittihad to a list of terrorism-related entities whose assets were frozen by an Executive Order. Bush Administration officials accused Al-Ittihad of links with Al Qaeda. The Administration did not publicly offer evidence supporting its allegations, but some officials asserted that links between AIAI and Al Qaeda date back to the U.S. presence in Somalia during Operation Restore Hope (1992-1994). This assertion, however, seems inconsistent with the reality on the ground at that time, according to some observers. Then, the dominant players in Mogadishu were the warlords and not Al-Ittihad. In early November 2001, federal authorities raided several Somali-owned money transfer businesses in the United States operated by Al-Barakaat Companies.

Source: Adapted by CRS. Cartographic Section, United Nations Department of Peacekeeping Operations, Map No. 3690 Rev. 7, January 2007.

Figure 2. Map of Somalia

The Bush Administration ordered the assets of Al-Barakaat frozen because of its alleged links to Al Qaeda. U.S. officials, however, later seemed to back off from their earlier assertion that AlBarakaat and individuals associated with the money transfer business sector are directly linked to Al Qaeda. In September 2002, U.S. officials cleared three Somalis and three Al-Barakaat branches accused of ties with Al Qaeda. The three individuals and businesses were removed from the U.S. Treasury Department list of terrorist supporters and their assets were also unfrozen. Nonetheless, the Bush Administration remains concerned about terrorist activities in Somalia, although no attacks against U.S. interests have been carried out by any known Somali groups. The United States has had no presence in Somalia since Washington pulled out of the peacekeeping operation in 1994. In September 2008, the European Court of Justice annulled the decision taken by the EU Council to freeze the assets of two Somalis and Al-Barakaat International Foundation of Sweden.

End Notes

[1] CRS interview with senior TFG officials and members of the Somali opposition in Kenya, May and August 2008.
[2] United Nations Political Office for Somalia (UNPOS), August 2008.
[3] CRS interview in Kenya with U.N. Special Envoy Ould-Abdallah, August 2008.
[4] CRS interview with a leader of the Islamic Courts, November 2008.
[5] "Young Somali Men Missing from Minneapolis," *International Herald Tribune*, November 27, 2008.
[6] "Routinely Targeted Attacks on Civilians in Somalia," *Amnesty International*, May 2008.
[7] CRS interviewed a number of journalists and human rights advocates in Kenya in 2007 and 2008. In November 2008, CRS met with a group of Somali human rights advocates, who fled Somalia for safety.
[8] CRS interviews with Somali officials, opposition leaders, and regional officials.
[9] Ted Dagne interviewed many Somalis in Dadaab refugee camp in Kenya in 2007-2008.
[10] http://new.unep.org/tsunami
[11] Ted Dagne interview with U.N. Special Envoy in Kenya, August 2008.
[12] Political program of the Alliance for the Re-Liberation of Somalia.
[13] Author interview with senior ICU official in late December 2006.
[14] Author interview with senior ICU official and regional sources in the Horn of Africa.
[15] Michael Gordon and Mark Mazzetti. "U.S. Used Base in Ethiopia to Hunt Al Qaeda," *New York Times*. February 23, 2007.
[16] http://news.bbc.co.uk/2/hi/africa/6273949.stm
[17] Communiqué of the African Union Peace and Security Council 69th Meeting, January 19, 2007.
[18] Peter Goodspeed, "Somalia Looking Like Pre-Taliban Afghanistan: U.S. Backed Warlords, Al Qaeda-Linked Thugs Kill Dozens" *National Post*, with files from News Services. May 16, 2006.
[19] The author met with several Members of Parliament and the TFG Foreign Minister in Kenya in August 2006.
[20] "Somali Islamic Courts Leader Comments on Domestic Situation, Future Outlook." Al-Ashraq Al-Awsat. June 6, 2006.
[21] The author had over 25 conversations between July 2006 and March 2007 with senior Islamic Courts officials and Somali residents in Mogadishu.

[22] *Foreign Broadcast Information Services (FBIS)*. "Islamists Regroup Their Forces After Ethiopian Preemptive Strike," May 17-23, 1999.

CHAPTER SOURCES

The following chapters have been previously published:

Chapter 1 – This is an edited, reformatted and augmented version of remarks delivered as a Statement of Michael Coulter, Principal Deputy Assistant Secretary of Defense for International Security Affairs, before the House Armed Services Committee, dated March 5, 2009.

Chapter 2 – This is an edited, reformatted and augmented version of remarks delivered as a Statement of Vice Admiral William E. Gortney, U.S. Navy Commander, U.S. Naval Armed Forces Central Command, before the House Armed Services Committee, dated March 5, 2009.

Chapter 3 – This is an edited, reformatted and augmented version of remarks delivered as a Statement of Ambassador Stephen D. Mull, before the House Armed Services Committee, dated March 5, 2009.

Chapter 4 - This is an edited, reformatted and augmented version of remarks delivered as a Statement of Karl Wycoff, Acting Deputy Assistant Secretary, Bureau of African Affairs, before the House Armed Services Committee, dated March 5, 2009.

Chapter 5 – This is an edited, reformatted and augmented version of a United States Congressional Research Service publication, Report Order Code R40081, dated February 6, 2009.

Chapter 6 – This is an edited, reformatted and augmented version of a United States Congressional Research Service publication, Report Order Code R40528, dated September 28, 2009.

Chapter 7 – This website information has been edited, reformatted and augmented from *http://www.skuld.com/upload/News%20and%20Publications/* Publications/Piracy/Somali%20Pirate%20Tactics%20Pamphlet%202008.pdf.

Chapter 8 - This is an edited, reformatted and augmented version of a United States Congressional Research Service publication, Report Order Code RL33911, dated February 18, 2009.

INDEX

C

D

E

F

G

H

I

R

S

T

U

V

W

Y